Not an Expert,
Just a Dad …
In this Crazy Game Called Life

By Jon Buzby

For my three sons … for making fatherhood all it's meant to be.

And to my wife … for making it happen in so many ways.

Not an Expert,
Just a Dad …
In this Crazy Game Called Life

PROLOGUE

When you sit back and think about it, life really is just like a game.

From the moment we enter this world we are coached by our parents, and then like any good coach does, we are left alone to make the on-field decisions for ourselves once we reach adulthood.

More often than not, in life we are like players on a team. Sometimes we have to play offense, like when we feel our child or spouse is wronged. Other times we are forced to defend, like when we screw up at work and try to talk our way out of it.

We also spend a good part of our life in the bleachers, just sitting back and watching time go by. It might be watching our children in the school play, attending a friend's wedding, or just sitting in a lawn chair at the family reunion — concession stand beer in hand — wondering where the time went.

A ballgame analogy can also be used when discussing the three basic needs in life: concession stands (food), stadiums (shelter) and uniforms (clothing).

I'll start with the first. I'm married to the most fabulous cook in the world. The only things different between Rachael Ray and my wife are a magazine cover, a syndicated television show and millions of dollars. My wife is even better looking (I think).

And yet, every night as I delve into another homemade dessert following a well-balanced, nutritious meal, I wonder if I could live a healthy life on three brownie sundaes a day. I'd consume less calories and fat than the so-called daily allowances, and would certainly make my wife's decision on what to cook for dinner easier. The only drawback I see is that I'd have to avoid seconds. Well, maybe just thirds.

But seriously, the horse-sized daily vitamins I take supposedly have more essential nutrients in them than I need for a week, so why wouldn't it work. I know, what about protein? Fortunately, I love melted peanut butter on my brownie sundaes.

And then there is shelter. We all supposedly want that white-picket fence wrapped around our homes like on "Leave it to Beaver." But when you think about it, what purpose does it really serve? Small dogs can crawl between the posts or under the rails, large dogs will jump over it, and it doesn't keep any rodents out. The pointed tops have to be sanded and painted annually and if I were to jump over it and come up short ... well, you get the picture. Or, if you are a man, admit it, you just winced and can feel my pain.

And finally ... clothing. Is there anything more different from generation to generation than fashion? About the only clothing style that hasn't changed since I got out of the cloth ones in the late 1960s, is disposable diapers. Like long hair or mullets on boys, baggy pants were in, then out, and now back in style again. Just with a lot more underwear showing. Clogs are back. Fortunately, Swatches have stayed out. And what's up with the furry snow boots on a sunny warm day? Lastly, does anyone — other than my wife — really care whether my clothes match when I arrive at work as long as I do my job?

The following chapters are a collection of fifty columns relating to parenting and living life with my three sons, who have a span of seventeen years between the first and the third. To provide a little clarity, my first son Alex is from a first marriage and born in 1992. Boys number two (Riley) and three (Tyler) are from my second, current, and last marriage, and were born in 2007 and 2008, respectively.

Some of what you'll read in the following pages offer opinions, others advice. And some you might not get anything out of it other than a chuckle or two. It's a hodgepodge of topics in no particular order so you can pick the book up and put it down without losing your spot. It's about life's ups and downs, and win or lose, the lessons learned along the way.

It's me playing my favorite position in this Crazy Game Called Life.

Now batting … Dad.

MY BOY BECOMES A MAN

Alex is my oldest son from a first marriage, and as many friends have pointed out over the years, my former wife and I get along better than many married couples. We'd like to think that's one of the reasons Alex has turned into a fine young man. We probably don't deserve the credit we think we do.

Alex's mom and I divorced when he was five years old. His biggest concern at the time was whether he could still get the Green Bay Packers dresser he had been promised before hearing the news. Ignorance is bliss.

From the time of the divorce until he was twelve, it was just the two of us when he stayed with me every other night, and I made sure he had my undivided attention. Whether we were doing homework, having a catch or walking to the ice-cream shop, it felt like that old television show, "The Courtship of Eddie's Father." I honestly think I spent more quality time with him than some fathers do with their kids who they live with fulltime.

I always made sure he had a hot meal for dinner and homemade pancakes before going to school. I even cut them until he was in middle school.

During his entire life from kindergarten until graduation he spent every other night at the other parent's home. We offered schedules more similar to children of other divorces, but he always said he liked it the way it was. And I guess it's really all he ever knew that he can remember. It was a routine he was comfortable with and liked, and that's what counts more than anything during a divorce.

I used to drive him to school every day, even on the mornings when he wasn't with me. I'd pick him up at his mom's and drive him to the bus stop. I didn't have to, but it was our time. Whether we talked about sports, school or nothing at all, it was time spent that I will always cherish.

There were challenges raising a child living in two different houses. Sometimes he'd forget to bring a school book to the right house or not have his sneakers on gym day. One time he left his headgear for the orthodontist appointment on his other nightstand.

But I always tried to go out of my way and never have him suffer just because his parents are divorced. And so there were a few late-night trips to his mom's house for this or that. During those trips, instead of being ticked that I was on the road when I could have been watching a big game or maybe should have been getting ready for bed, I tried to think of all the other parts of his life he handled so well, divorce or not.

His mother and I are both remarried and have young kids with our second spouses. Instead of being a big brother, Alex is more like an uncle to all of them. And he's a great one. He has adapted to having two stepparents and is blessed to have two great ones.

Sure, there have been bumps along the way. We've fought over study habits, keeping his room clean, going over his cell phone minutes, and whether or not he'd drive his own car, mine or keep riding the bus.

I've accepted the fact that he'd rather talk to his mom about certain things — girls, girls, girls — just like I did with mine. And that just because I did something one way growing up doesn't mean he will or should do it that way.

I often found myself balancing the scale between being one of my son's favorite people and being his father. It was often hard to be both. Hopefully he'd give me a passing grade.

He's now a college graduate and on his own. I knew he was officially an adult when I called to chat one night and he told me he was moving into his second apartment the following week and didn't need my help at all. It made me proud ... and admittedly a little sad.

When people ask me how he's doing, I reply, "He's happy, healthy and employed."

I couldn't be prouder of him or happier for him.

RILEY ARRIVES

Picture this: television with remote control, three cell phones with chargers, two laptop computers, printer, wireless internet access, leather recliner, adjustable bed with adjustable lighting, and a butler on call. Sounds like heaven, right?

Actually, it was the labor and delivery room. And the butler was actually a nurse who, rightfully so, didn't give a damn about my needs.

On this particular morning, my pregnant wife had her weekly doctor's appointment and I got a call from her at the office telling me, "It's time!" My response: "Time for what?" I'm confident I'll live that one down, eventually.

She was on the way to the hospital. A quick juggle of my schedule, a gathering of materials and I'm out the door like Batman when the commissioner calls.

We arrive at the hospital only to be told the entire induction period could take more than twenty-four hours — I obviously wasn't paying attention during that discussion in the childbirth class — and I should go home and gather some things. Of course, we have no bag packed, no plan for the dogs and the car seat only recently was taken out of the box (but I have yet to figure out how to disconnect it from the base). I look for something that the baby can wear when he or she comes home and all I can find is a New York Jets outfit that will fit perfectly in about three years.

I stumble up to the hospital room carrying enough bags to spend the month and enter only to find my wife grading papers. She sees me unpack my laptop and glares at me with a look that screams, "No, you are not really going to write a column about this are you?" The screams from the next room quickly divert her attention elsewhere and so I settle back in the recliner and begin to hunt and peck.

I decide not to complain about having to watch the Food Network instead of ESPN. Instead, I try to find ways to make my wife more comfortable. "Would you like part of my cheesesteak with your ice chips?" I'm confident the pounding of the computer keys are not bothering her. Besides, the thumping of the baby's heartbeat from the monitor hooked up to her are drowning them out.

Wait! Baby? Heartbeat? Oh my gosh! My life is about to change drastically. Foreverrrrrrrr!

As my wife drifts off to sleep (and I gain control of the remote), all of a sudden, all those things that I wanted to get done before the baby arrives aren't so important. The essentials are all set. The bassinette is put together (putting baby furniture together is a column for another time), I'm told there are plenty of clothes for the newborn without the Jets logo, and the nursery is painted and ready to go.

So instead, my attention turns where it should - to my wife, the mother of our soon-to-be-born child, the woman who not only will give birth to this beautiful creature, but will nurture it for a lifetime. Anyone who tells you that parenting ends when your kid turns eighteen has yet to raise a child to that point. Parenting starts at conception and never ends, just ask your parents.

Despite having lived through childbirth once as a dad, the experience isn't making this second go-round any easier. I feel ecstatic nervousness like never before, fear like only an expecting father can undergo and, in many ways, a helpless sentiment of wanting to help, yearning to ease the pain, yet knowing all I can do is support. That's where I'm at right now. The contractions don't seem to be often or very painful — I know, easy for me to say — and yet with every twitch from the bed next to me, I jump from my seat asking if she's alright.

11

We are seven hours in so far, with what could be another entire day to go. They tell you in all those childbirth classes that it's a long process, but what they don't tell you is everything that can go on during that process - for us dads, anyway. I've decided those childbirth classes need a dad's point of view, too. Nobody in that class told me I'd be across the street shopping at the baby store for nursing bras. Or, when I went to get lunch I should have eaten in the cafeteria rather than tease my wife with it as she chomped on ice chips.

So now it's time to sit and wait and wonder. Boy or girl? Big or small? Perfectly healthy?

After a restless night's sleep cramped up on a bed built for the skinniest guy in the world smashed against what I'm convinced is the largest cold window in the place, I awoke to find out that my wife dilated from four to eight centimeters in about two hours. She is resting quietly with the epidural fully in effect, laughing under her breath at anyone not wanting it. We are now on our third nurse, each younger than the previous one, but none as young as the first doctor who saw her. All of a sudden I feel like a grandfather rather than an expecting father.

Anyone who has ever had surgery or any type of care in a hospital and isn't completely impressed by the knowledge and skills of the medical personnel must spend their entire time there completely under anesthesia. They are truly amazing.

Several hours later our son, Riley, was born with no complications. After the cord was cut (by the doctor, not me) and he was cleaned up, weighed and measured, I remembered that I had brought a camera to take pictures as soon as he popped out. I called relatives from my cell phone and emailed friends from my laptop with the good news (just like on Walton's Mountain when those kids were born, I'm sure).

And then the hustle and bustle of the forty-eight hours after birth began. We were moved to a new room, I debated how to get more visitors in than allowed, and I quickly got over the fact that the television screen

12

was smaller than my laptop computer and there was no remote. My wife was roommate-less the first night only to be joined by a woman who gave birth to her fifth child, which is four more than my wife will have, according to her as of today.

My wife was disappointed that she'd have to stay for one night so you can imagine her dismay when she found out it was two. That meant two sleepless nights. For her, that is. One of my friends emailed me the day after Riley was born and asked how the first night went and I replied, "I slept soundly all nine hours at home, thanks for asking!" I was smart enough not to mention that conversation to my wife.

I made one more trip back to the baby store for binkies, the onesies that snap on the side and yes, more nursing bras. But you know what, this time I didn't seem to care. I was beaming as I went through the store. Now that I know it's a boy I even had a boatload of sports apparel in the shopping cart but wisely decided it looked better on the shelf than it would on my credit card.

Wow, it all happened so fast. Nine months flew by (according to me, not my wife) and now I'm a dad again. I hold him in my arms and think that this little creature is counting on me to give him everything he needs to be happy and healthy. What a major responsibility on my shoulders. But truth be told, I wouldn't want that responsibility on any other dad in the world. He's all mine.

I know there will be sleepless nights, long car rides to lull him to sleep and countless loads of laundry.

I'll get pooped on, peed on and puked on. Even that will be worth it.

There will be books to read. At first I'll pick the ones I prefer to read but eventually he'll have his favorites and they will quickly become mine.

That will be followed by hours of "Barney" and "Sesame Street," locking the house down from top to bottom when he starts crawling, putting that first tricycle together only to realize his feet don't reach the pedals yet, and then eventually his first day of school when I'll be more nervous than he'll be.

But I wouldn't trade these moments for anything in the world, except more just like them.

I know from raising one child that the days he'll want to spend time with me are numbered, and I don't plan to waste one of them.

TYLER IS NOT A FISH

Dear Tyler,

Welcome to the world. A world that, quite frankly, an outside observer might second guess whether you'd want to enter or not.

We just elected our first African-American president, which is a good thing. But we're still fighting wars a world away, which is a bad thing. There was no turmoil inside Mommy.

Riley isn't quite sure what to make of you, but I can tell you that he was more interested in the fish tank in the hospital than he was meeting you.

When Riley was born, I managed to write a column before he was two hours old. But with you, now more than a week old, the words just aren't flowing.

It has nothing to do with a lack of excitement about your arrival. Just ask your mom; the smile that she saw on my face when I first held you looked exactly like the one that she has now seen just twice, and will never see again.

And what I mean by that is, barring a miracle in science, you will probably be the last grandchild on either side of our families. Unfortunately for you, the honor reaps no monetary rewards. In fact, I better remind both sets of grandparents to update their wills.

The doctor declared all nine pounds of you "a third-grader" when you popped into the world and your mom yelled out, "I'm done." If your mother had had her way, I would have been "fixed" before you were cleaned up.

Riley was shocked when he walked in the door on your first day home. I think he would have preferred to see a fish tank. He didn't realize that you and Mommy came home from the hospital as a package deal.

I've now remembered that I completely forgot how to change a newborn. That whole circumcision and umbilical cord strategy is getting old. I'm ready for your first "man poop."

At the same time, part of me never wants you to get a day older. Watching your oldest brother drive himself to school for the first time this past week and hearing Riley put together two- and three-word sentences makes me realize just how fast time flies.

And maybe that's my hesitation in writing this column ... because I know it's my last one about becoming a daddy again. Watching you grow up knowing I won't see these stages again is something I'm hesitant to look forward to. As I watched Riley go through stages during the past twenty-two months, one of the many things that made it so much fun for Mommy and me was because we knew we'd eventually have you to compare. Who would walk first, talk the most, and just how much alike would you be?

Now with you, son, it's the end of the line. Yours is the second and last umbilical cord that will ever fall off in this house (hopefully the dog won't eat this one). We won't store the bassinette, port-a-crib or infant car seat this time around, we'll give them away. And if we can ever get your older brother to stop using his binky, when you're done with yours, they'll get tossed.

Your mother is already planning a yard sale for the spring of 2010, which, by the way, is the same year that your oldest brother will graduate from high school. A milestone, like him driving, I never thought would be in sight.

My hope is that you are close to both your brothers. One will be more like an uncle to you at first, and the other, who will double as your

16

sparring partner growing up, might eventually become your very best friend.

Unfortunately for you, even after two tries I haven't perfected fatherhood. I'll probably offer to have the sex talk with you about three years after you've learned it all. I'm sure I'll ground you for life more than once. And my guess is your mom will again tell me at some point that it's more important that you learn how to write with your correct hand than pitch with your left.

But for the last time in my life, if I screw something up I can't say, "I'll get it right with the next one."

It's a position I knew I would be in when we found out you were on the way, but like your oldest brother driving a car or your other brother talking, it's a time I never thought would get here.

But now that you have arrived, I awake each morning with a smile on my face, knowing that I'm once again blessed with a beautiful baby boy; a third son; my golf foursome complete.

Just like with your brothers, your mother and I will do everything in our power to give you everything you need to live a happy and healthy life. Some of those things you'll want, while others you won't understand. Just rest assured that every decision we make will be, in our opinion, in your best interest.

Despite the sometimes crazy world we live in, this outside observer is glad you're here. So are countless family members and friends. Now that you are here, sit back and enjoy the ride. I plan to savor every second of every stage, one last fabulous time.

And don't worry, eventually Riley will accept the fact that you aren't a fish.

GREAT BALLS ON FIRE

My male friends told me I was nuts (no pun intended).

My wife made sure to include a bag of frozen peas — which are my least favorite vegetable — on her weekly grocery list.

The day had finally arrived. As we drove to the doctor's office, I saw a huge billboard for the Powerball just as the lyrics to "Great Balls of Fire" blared from the radio.

I was nobly heading in for what many assured me was a very minor procedure - a vasectomy.

As I lay on the operation table in all my glory, wide awake, getting ready to eliminate any chance of me having more kids, ironically the subject of the now-infamous octuplets came up among the medical staff.

The doctor said he heard that the mother was asking for millions in appearance fees. And just as I questioned whether I was making the right decision or maybe, just maybe, should try to father eight kids and become a millionaire ... I heard a snip, snip, and just like that my dream for potential millions was snapped like the branch on my family tree.

And just like that, about twenty minutes after I kissed my wife before I headed in for the procedure, I was back out in the lobby ready to head home. She had barely opened her magazine.

She couldn't believe it was over. She had what seemed like a million questions, and I felt like I had a million eyes staring at me waiting for answers. I kindly asked if we could wait and discuss it on the way home. Her reply: "Why? I'm sure you'll be writing about it anyway."

After driving over what seemed like every bump in the state, we finally arrived home and I headed for the recliner with my bag of frozen peas (a wonderful suggestion, by the way).

In my wife's circle of female friends, I am a hero. Apparently the procedure for a woman to have her tubes tied is far more complicated, with a multi-week recovery that is similar to that of any invasive surgery.

For me, my brief recovery will be spent being waited on hand and foot (doctor's orders). Oh, and I'll get closer to that bag of frozen peas than I ever dreamed possible.

Our discussion about me having this procedure started during my wife's pregnancy with Tyler. And then was brought up again before he was even cleaned up and measured. She more or less said, "The ball is in your court, Honey."

Two months prior to the procedure, I had the required consultation. It lasted less than five minutes. The doctor basically told me how the procedure goes, what the recovery is and, by the way, you'll be finished fathering children. Maybe this consultation should be a requirement to play in the NBA.

I was very open about having it done, even though I just couldn't come around to calling my mother and announcing it to her. I sent an email to my colleagues, women included, telling them I'd be out for three days having some minor surgery but would return to work with a higher-pitched voice and a guarantee never to become a father again.

My one male colleague replied, "In your case, I guess it really is considered a small surgery." Another female friend said it was "the best gift a husband could give his wife for Valentine's Day." As I sit here with the bag of frozen peas, all of a sudden, over-priced roses seem like a bargain.

But seriously, having watched my wife go through childbirth twice, I'm convinced that if we men had to give birth, the life process would have ended years ago.

Every couple approaches birth control differently. I just thought all you men out there considering a vasectomy might want to hear it directly from someone who has gone through it, rather than hearing it from your doctor (who gets paid thousands to put you through it and probably has not had it), or your wife's friends (who tell you their husbands did it with no problem, while their spouses are in a different room).

I still don't like the word minor, or any synonym of it, being used when referring to my procedure in particular, but compared to giving birth, it really isn't a big deal. For my wife, it would have been. It's the least I could do.

Of course, I now hate peas more than ever.

FIRST DAY JITTERS

Most of us have had the painful affliction that I'll call butterflyous jitteritis. Some of us still do. The layman's term is first-day-of-school jitters, or simply put, butterflies. And it can be before any new experience, not just the first day of school. Symptoms include nausea, loss of appetite, sweating and wanting absolutely nothing to do with donning the new school clothes and heading out to the bus stop.

Every year from kindergarten until about fifth grade, my mother had to coax me out the door as I battled my own version of butterflyous jitteritis. Of course, by nine in the morning I was cured. That is, until the next morning. This went on for about three days at the beginning of the school year. And not just heading into kindergarten, but every year until about fourth grade and then again on my first days of junior high and then high school. At that point I thought I was cured … until my first day of college.

My mom was like a butterfly tamer. She knew just the right way to handle those critters and somehow managed to get me to school with very few tears and even an appetite by lunchtime (breakfast was out of the question). The only problem is I just don't know how she did it. As many tricks as she passed on to me to use when raising my children, I never learned how to tame butterflies.

But here's my thinking …

Dads tend to be tough on that first day of school (either that or still in bed). "What are you nervous about? It's only school. Get on the bus!" That wouldn't have helped me and I'm sure wouldn't help most kids. My mom seemed to have that knack of making sure those early-morning butterflies disappeared by late morning. She didn't get upset — although my guess is it was tearing her up inside to see me so upset — and she acted like being nervous was perfectly normal. She even told me stories about how she used to get nervous.

Forcing your child to eat breakfast only makes it worse. I went to school breakfast-less for those first days every year and somehow survived. I think I ate my first breakfast at college on the fourth day. Maybe if you can just get a glass of juice in your child before she leaves, that will at least get something in her stomach. Or let her choose what to eat. Somehow a donut on a queasy stomach sounds much better than scrambled eggs and sausage or pancakes smothered in butter and syrup.

Remind your child how much her friends are hoping to see her and how they are probably nervous, too. You might even suggest a phone call to a friend just for reassurance that everyone is nervous and they'll all get through it together.

At the end of the first day, remember that the second day might not be much better first thing in the morning and help prepare your child for that, too. Remind her that if she's nervous again, just to think back to today and how once she got to school and around her friends she was fine. There is no guarantee that this will work — it didn't for me, just ask my mom — but at least it's better than pretending butterflies won't reappear.

So to all you kids out there whose parents just said, "Here, read this," take it from me, the hardest part of overcoming butterflyous jitteritis is getting out the front door. Once you're at school, you'll be fine. And for a change, no matter what they are serving for lunch, you'll be hungry for it.

WHAT IS QUALITY TIME

Is being home under the same roof with your kids but in a separate room quality time? How about going to church? What if at the family picnic you are all talking to relatives instead of each other?

What exactly is quality time? All parents talk about spending it with our kids, but do we really? How often does the tall grass, dirty laundry or game of the week take precedence over quality time with our children? I'm sure if you really think about it, more often than not.

In this "on the go" world with many families having two working parents and kids in multiple activities, is it even possible to have quality family time?

How much quality time did you spend with your children last weekend? I figure there was probably about twenty-five hours of time that all of you were awake and under the same roof. How much of it was spent as quality time? Not just together somewhere, but real honest-to-goodness quality time?

To me, quality time must include both of the following criteria:

It must be time spent together between you and at least one of your children doing something at least one of you enjoys, but preferably both. Remember, sometimes quality time is doing something with someone because they like it even if you don't.

There needs to be some sort of conversation taking place, not necessarily nonstop, but at least an opportunity for it, and it can be one way if the situation warrants.

So based on my criteria, quality time is not riding in the car with your son with the radio blaring, you on the cell phone and him playing on his favorite electronic device. However, if you turn off the radio for the ride, hang up the cell, put away the video game and chat about what's going on in school, all of a sudden you have quality time.

Doing homework together does not count as quality time since neither of you really want to be doing it, but reading a bedtime story or playing a board game does. Cooking dinner while your kids play video games at the kitchen table does not, but making a dessert together does.

Quality time wouldn't be outside doing yard work with your child on opposite sides of the house. That is until you take a break to admire your work and talk about his or her latest crush.

Going to watch your child play a youth soccer game is one of the best ways a parent can be supportive. However, while he is playing, you aren't together and you can't talk, so neither criterion of quality time is met. However, talking about the game on the car ride home does count as quality time.

Quality time is not the time spent after your child has run off to the swings or sliding board, but rather the walk to and from the playground talking about anything and everything.

One of my favorite things I used to do with my son when he was a toddler was go to the doughnut shop on Saturday mornings. We would sit and have a doughnut and something to drink and then drive to the local marina and walk the docks admiring the boats. It took us about two hours.

We were together doing something we both enjoyed and had some fascinating conversations, including some that wouldn't make sense to anyone but us. Now that was quality time!

My guess is he doesn't remember much of it, but I'll never forget it. And you know what? When we got back home after those two hours, the grass wasn't any higher than when we left.

It's a little easier finding ways to spend quality time when your kids are young. But as they get older, it becomes more difficult to find something that meets the quality-time criteria. Between jobs, chores, volunteer duties, schoolwork and kids' activities, it's a real challenge to find opportunities for quality time.

One of these days I'll drop my son off at high school. And my guess is he won't want to stop at the donut shop on the way.

Don't let time slip away.

AN EARLY SCOUTING REPORT

My youngest son turned one a few weeks ago, and earlier this week he gave me my first indication that a career in baseball might be a possibility.

It was tubby time and all of a sudden the rubber duck flew through the air and landed on my lap, soaking me from head to toe. Now, while most moms would be furious at this point, we dads, of course, are prouder than ever.

I yelled frantically for my wife to come upstairs. She dropped whatever she was doing and barreled up the steps to find there was no blood, not one tear drop and no bumps or bruises. In fact, we were both smiling ear to ear. Once she knew we were both perfectly healthy, she was not happy.

Once she calmed down, her first question was, "Well, coach, which hand did he throw it with?" A look of fluster went over me. I didn't know, and as of now he has yet to re-attempt the duck toss. Or any other toss for that matter.

So this made me wonder if there are other things I should be doing to help hone his athletic skills.

He loves to watch balls roll around. And so I make sure to roll them to him often. He stops about one in ten. But the one he stops, he gets cheers as if he just won the big game. And, of course, the former soccer goalkeeper in me occasionally rolls a few to his side just to see his reaction. Right now, it's just a frustrated smirk as it rolls past him out of reach.

He has a little hoop that is stuck to the side of the tub. During bath time I toss in the little balls that came with it. His reaction? He rips the hoop off and dumps the balls out for me to toss back in. Once in a great while he'll grab a ball and dunk it. I'm confident he's well on his way to NBA All-Star weekend.

One of his favorite toys is what a musician calls a maraca. I call it a small golf club that makes noise when you swing it. Whenever he has it in his hands I put balls on the floor — not real golf balls ... yet — and try to get him to swing at them. He'll hit one in fifty. My guess is Tiger Woods was a bit more successful at this age.

One of his favorite games I call NASCAR. He gets on his scooter and I push him around the house doing laps through various rooms. He shrieks with excitement and we even have some soft crashes. It's a game we usually save for when mommy is at the grocery store. I think in his mind he's even questioning how difficult it is to make four left turns through the kitchen, dining room and living room.

The bottom line is nothing I'm doing now is going to prepare him for the big leagues in any sport. Most likely he'll get as close to being a pro as me, which was nowhere close. But it is fun dreaming. For me, that is. He'd probably just as soon be left alone to play with his boats in the tub.

Speaking of which, time to go check out the American Power Boat Association website.

A POSITIVE TO VOMIT

The other night, my wife and I were awakened by the dreaded sound of vomit spewing through the baby monitor. Well, not literally, but you get the point.

We raced into the baby's room knowing we were too late to salvage the bedding or pajamas. After the first cleanup, what followed were three more duplicate episodes, four loads of laundry, and a sleepless night for both of us.

I'm not sure there's a worse feeling for a parent than when your baby gets sick all over himself and then stares at you with that quizzical "this never happened in the womb" look.

But then again, we were quickly reminded as the stomach virus ripped through our house that it really doesn't matter whether your child is a baby, toddler or teenager, seeing them suffer through the pain and sometimes confusion of throwing up is one of the worst feelings for a parent. And we saw it happen plenty of times last week, and I even participated myself.

But why is it that mothers rarely get the bug? I never, ever remember my mother being sick to the point that she was quarantined to bed and not able to care for us. My father, just like me, would have been perfectly capable of taking care of the household while my mom recovered in bed. But like me, never seemed to be put in that situation.

I succumbed to the virus two nights after Tyler, six hours before Riley, and then had a relapse three days before my teenager succumbed to the bug. My wife? Not a touch of it as of today, four full days after we aired the house out to the point of being able to see my breath.

When I asked her why she thinks she avoided it, she replied that she doesn't have time to be bedridden. And my guess is my mother, and probably my wife's mom, and both of their mothers, felt the same way.

The night I was quarantined to my room was the night Riley decided it was his turn. The first upchuck episode was similar to Tyler's: barf, lay in it, wake up confused, scream for help, and then look up in bewilderment when mommy arrives. But at least he was able to aim for, and hit, the bucket the rest of the night.

Forever my wife has claimed she can't handle blood or vomit. Yet, just as she did a few nights earlier when the coffee table got in the way of our newest walker's head, she managed to handle, without flinching, the latest household drama of seeing the day's earlier meal reproduced in chunks. It's just what moms do.

Vomit aside, kids are so cute when all they want is to be held when they are sick. And they're even more adorable when you holding them is the instant cure, even if it's only until the next bucket-grabbing episode.

When your kids don't understand and can't control what's going on with their own bodies, the touch of yours seems to be a better remedy than any dry crackers or toast ever could be. It doesn't matter if that touch happens while you are staring down at a bed sheet counting peas or holding a forehead while leaning over the porcelain goddess (something I "fondly" remember my mother doing every single time I got sick – Dad must have been quarantined).

Getting sick isn't fun for us adults. Just imagine our kids' feeling of not knowing when it's coming, what's happening, or how to fix it other than to roll away from it and scream for help. I guess there's a reason we have forgotten experiencing it ourselves when we were that young. Or maybe we subconsciously really don't, and that's why we are able to handle it when it's our kids.

29

Cleaning up after sick kids gets old real fast. Just ask my wife. But something that never gets old is the cure from the touch of a loved one. For our kids who are sick, it comes from us parents. And for us parents watching our kids get sick, it comes from knowing our kids will calm down in our arms after a violent bout with the stomach virus. The spreading of germs never seems to matter at that point.

The stomach virus eventually went away from our house. However, the comforting feeling of need it created has not.

UNDERWEAR IS NOT A GIFT

Moms all over the country are probably scratching their heads wondering what to get that special dad in the household for Valentine's Day. Unlike moms, for dads it's pretty easy. A bundle of flowers and dinner out usually does the trick. Dancing is a bonus and breakfast in bed not a bad idea. Or maybe just an hour or two of quiet time sans kids. But what do you moms get your testosterone-loaded husband on this most romantic of days?

I'm going to suggest a gift-giving rule of thumb to follow so that your male mate will appreciate you, love you even more, and most importantly, think you are the most romantic person in the world when he opens your gift on Cupid's big day. Oh ... and here's another hint: It might not be a bad idea to remind him about this special holiday a week ahead of time.

It's really quite simple: Buy him something he wants, can and will use, will enjoy, and that he'll always remember you giving him as a gift, even if he can't remember the occasion.

Actually, this rule of thumb can be used for anniversaries, too. My wife and I recently celebrated our fifth anniversary. My gift to her was earrings with the December gemstone representing the month we were married. I know, what a guy! Romantic as heck. I rock.

Her gift to me was a satellite radio. My wife rocks! I realize the gift from her was not romantic at all, but both gifts follow my simple gift-giving rule of thumb and we each loved our gift from the other.

So ladies, keeping this rule of thumb in mind, please don't buy him boxers with hearts on them, a box of chocolate or reservations at your favorite restaurant. Instead of breakfast in bed, he'd much rather have breakfast alone at the table where he can read the paper while eating and not spill coffee all over the sheets.

You have to think outside the box. And here's one more hint - most things we guys want for these special occasions don't come in fancy boxes. Every time I get in my car and turn on my satellite radio, I think of our anniversary and how thoughtful my wife was to know how much I'd appreciate access to multiple national sports talk shows and commercial-free music stations.

The gift doesn't have to be expensive or sentimental or come with an explanation because the right gift won't need one. Maybe buy him tickets to see his favorite professional team play and if not with you, maybe his good friend. How about a membership to the local health club or a car accessory? Just note I said accessory, like the satellite radio, not necessity, like four tires? None of these probably sound romantic, but trust me, he will think it is because you put his feelings first when shopping.

More "no-no's" include a tool of any type, because we take that as you wanting something fixed. Don't send anything to his office that ends with "gram," and don't buy tickets to some sappy movie.

How about a free round of golf, his favorite band's most recent CD or a bottle of his favorite adult beverage?

Just make sure to remember my rule of thumb: Buying him a pair of boxers with hearts on them means about as much to him as you unwrapping a vacuum on Valentine's Day.

WHEN THE CAT'S AWAY ...

My wife recently went on "vacation" to Florida with my two youngest boys for a week to visit her folks. It was a long week for everyone involved, maybe especially my father-in-law, who instead of the morning news and "Walker: Texas Ranger" reruns was forced to watch "Barney" every morning.

But during my hiatus from my wife and boys — thank goodness for work — I learned a lot about myself, my life and my family.

Despite not having any crying kids in the house, I slept through the night exactly zero times. I went to the same amount of happy hours I usually do when they are home (zero). I didn't meet any friends for lunch. And for whatever reason, instead of watching sports around the clock, when it was couch time — normally spent with my wife by my side after both boys are in bed — I still watched the same "Cheers" reruns we always do. And I still laughed out loud at all the funny parts, just without my wife glaring at me with a quizzical look on her face because I've heard the punch lines hundreds of times.

But here are a few things I learned while living by myself for a week, or maybe just forgot from my bachelor days.

We don't really need to fold our underwear before putting it away. It all goes on the same and nobody sees it.

The television can stay on all night and it won't blow up.

Nobody really cares if I put those useless decorative pillows on the bed during the day.

Heck, for that matter, I didn't even really need to make the bed. I only did because I was convinced the bed-making fairy would rat me out if I didn't.

Crumbs in the bed don't attract ants. At least I didn't see any.

The oven is easily replaced by a delivery boy's knock at the door.

If you leave the snow on the driveway long enough, it eventually melts.

A wet towel left on the bathroom floor is easily replaced by a fresh one out of the closet when it's shower time.

Dinners are much, much better and less expensive when my wife makes them.

There is no dishwasher-emptying fairy. It must be my wife who does it.

And that goes for making my morning coffee, too.

There should be labels on the corners of bedsheets. Something like: If you lay face up in your bed, put this corner of the sheet at the foot of the bed to your right.

I also realized from the pictures my wife sent me via email and from talking to Riley on the phone that missing a week is like missing a month at their ages.

Riley talked to me nonstop on the phone about his train ride, plane ride, the garbage tractor and the golf cart. Oh, and the lizards he chased all week. "They were fun," he said.

Tyler went from looking like a newborn to a real baby in less than a week.

I also realized that just when I thought I had felt every emotion possible as a father, I added one to my top three list when Riley came running toward me in the airport screaming, "Daddy, Daddy, Daddy," as if he hadn't seen me in a year instead of it being just a short week.

Or, I guess I must admit, a very, very long week.

Dorothy said it best in the "Wizard of Oz": "There's no place like home." And I realize more than ever that my home is at its best when my entire family is in it.

FEELING OLD AT CHRISTMAS

If you are honest with yourself — and like your job as much as I do — you have to admit that as wonderful as the Christmas holiday season is, going back to work for us parents and school for the kids is sort of a respite from the hustle and bustle that accompany the holiday season.

During the holidays I tend to nap instead of exercise, eat thirds instead of seconds, and despite tripling my daily caloric intake, still find plenty of excuses to visit the donut shop every morning. And it's too cold to bike there.

Despite heading into my ten-day vacation with a full head of gray hair and a waistline several inches larger than desired, this holiday more than any other was the one when I really realized — or maybe just accepted — that at forty-two I'm no longer a spring chicken.

It started when I offered to take my seventeen-year-old son Christmas shopping so he could buy gifts for his parents, stepparents and siblings. His reply: "Thanks, but I'm finished shopping for everyone, including my girlfriend." He followed that declaration up with an announcement that he wanted to voluntarily attend all family holiday gatherings this year. At that point, for fear of the answer, I dared not ask him if he still believed in Santa Claus.

And as if my son's adult-like holiday actions weren't enough of a blow to my ageless ego, I made the leap and purchased a minivan. And no, it is not for my wife to cart the kids around like you would think, but instead for me.

36

As my toddler grows into a little boy and the infant becomes a toddler, coupled with my teenager's new desire to spend time with his family, I quickly realized that the only thing my compact sedan was good for was daycare drop-off. So I figured if I had to upsize, I might as well do it practically. That and the fact a Hummer was out of my price range.

Despite being teased by friends and family — Alex declared it a loser cruiser as he and my wife sat at the kitchen table creating a list of every senior citizen we know who owns one — the practicality of my practical people mover, or PPM as I refer to it in conversation to sound hip, became evident during our two out-of-state day trips over the holidays.

Less than an hour into its first voyage I watched through the rearview mirror as my wife maneuvered around chasing binkies, fetching toys, reading stories and serving food and drinks. Without her knowing, I quickly snapped a picture of her playing stewardess and sent it via text message to all the PPM naysayers. I even posted it on Facebook. That is, until she discovered it.

Around town, the ease of getting the kids in and out of the PPM was remarkable compared to the bending, stretching and banging of heads that had become routine in the smaller car. I figure the extra money I'm spending on the gas-guzzling PPM will more than offset what would have eventually been spent at the chiropractor.

The third and final event that proved to me I'm getting older happened when I met two of my best friends from high school for our annual holiday breakfast.

Typically the visit is spent re-hashing times from the good 'ol days of high school. But, not this time. The only mention of any classmate was a brief chat about the one member of our foursome who could not be with us, and there wasn't one recollection of any past highlight reel-worthy (in our minds) sports plays or other moments from nearly three decades ago.

In fact, our breakfast banter frighteningly sounded like one our parents — all who own PPMs by the way — might have. How are the kids?

37

How's the job? Can you believe our thirtieth reunion is next year? I haven't talked to so-and-so in years.

We ate, chatted and then had to rush back to family-related responsibilities, each of us in a family-type car we always swore we'd never own.

As I put my PPM in drive, made a quick stop at the gas station and began my journey home to start taking down Christmas lights, I sighed, and finally accepted the fact that not only am I not getting any younger, but this holiday season, I seemed to have matured — that sounds so much hipper than aged — more than any other.

SANTA DELIVERS A VIRUS

Our Christmas holiday started with a family-wide visit from the stomach virus before Santa even got near the chimney. We asked Santa to wrap a solution for teaching a toddler how to know when he's going to vomit so he can at least be within arm's reach of the toilet.

Things only got worse.

Just as everyone's bathroom visits became normal again, surgery to repair a tennis elbow followed for this one-armed typist who never realized before that changing diapers really is a two-handed job, as are several other tasks previously considered menial. Have you ever tried to put on a pair of socks or tie your shoes with one hand?

I finally declared myself useless, several hours after my wife already had.

I learned the hard way that painkillers and the aroma of the annual Christmas Eve seven-fish dinner my wife prepares don't mix well. But for every shrimp and scallop I chose to forgo, down the hatch a chocolate chip cookie went. After all, I had to maintain my strength.

Christmas morning was a flurry of strewn wrapping paper, with Riley just as interested in cleaning up the bows as he was opening the next gift. If we had kept his pace the twelfth day of Christmas would have been spent opening his last gift instead of drumming. Hundreds of dollars later, his favorite gift was the car from the dollar store that I stepped on and shattered before lunchtime.

The day after Christmas, our oldest son had a nice trip planned to New York City on the train with friends. It was on that morning, probably before Santa was finished the last gulp of his annual post-event glass of spiked eggnog, when I got the phone call I had been dreading since the day my role in the car changed from supervising driver to passenger: "Dad, I've been in an accident."

Thanks to airbag technology and this generation's most important lesson learned from my generation — seat belts do save lives — he and his friend escaped without a scratch and a lesson about early-morning slippery roads. But that gem-of-a-find car I found on the used car lot less than two months ago was going to be towed to its final resting place. With no collision insurance on the high-mileage car, my long-term investment became shorter with every turn of the tow crank.

Convincing your teenager that his life isn't over with the loss of his recently-purchased car — with a brand-new radio installed the day before the crash — is like trying to explain to a toddler that his favorite teddy bear will come out of the washer unscathed before bedtime. But after hearing, "The important thing is nobody was hurt," from everyone he spoke to about the accident and several stories from his uncles about their car mishaps that involved hospital stays, he's finally coming around to the realization that not only will his life go on, but in fact, it actually could have ended.

Watching him stare at his car being towed away is a memory I'll never forget, both his reaction as it disappeared around the corner and my relief that he lived to agonizingly watch it.

Later that same day, our holiday gathering with my side of the family was highlighted by Riley jumping off the couch and hurting his foot. If you've ever seen a toddler limp, you can't help but chuckle at just how cute it looks. But in the middle of the night when he wanted to limp out of the crib because his foot pain had returned, all of a sudden, like the medicine, the cuteness had worn off.

By this point of the holiday vacation, a mere two days after Santa had scooted back up our chimney, my wife and I sat in bed wide awake watching television after delivering another dose of medicine to Riley and

40

plunging Tyler's nose so he could breathe (his cold was so minor it didn't warrant a mention). We couldn't help but wonder what might go wrong next and whether we should strip the house of Christmas decorations to prevent anything else bad from happening.

As I was pondering whether I could climb a ladder with one arm to take the outdoor lights down, a commercial for the Ronald McDonald House appeared on the television screen like the timing of the ghosts in "A Christmas Carol." The ad was seeking donations so that families could temporarily live close to their children suffering from cancer in local hospitals.

It was at that very moment, with all three of our boys snuggled safely in bed suffering from only a case of the sniffles, a minor childhood injury and a temporarily broken heart caused by a pile of scrap metal, when we realized despite some unexpected bumps on the holiday sleigh ride, Santa managed to navigate it all and still deliver us the greatest gift of all.

GAME OVER

"Dad, I think I'm going to skip baseball season so I can work to earn enough money to buy a car."

A high school teacher of mine once said it best that kids miss out on stuff because they have to work so they can have a car, and the only real reason they need a car is so they can get to work.

Now my high school-age son was thinking the same thing the other night on the way home from basketball practice. This was the same son who preferred to watch baseball over cartoons. The son I proudly watched hit his first home run last spring.

And now I have to wonder if it was his last?

You might recall he totaled his first car over the holidays and, unfortunately for him, is learning the insurance lesson most of us already know. The car insurance companies don't care how nice of a kid you are or how good your grades can be, your rates are going to go up significantly once you've been in an accident that the police claim you caused. And it doesn't matter if Mother Nature making the roads slippery was really the cause or not, at least not in Delaware.

Giving up a favorite childhood activity is an issue all parents will face at some point. If it's not a sport, it might be piano or ballet lessons, Scouts, or maybe an activity in the church.

If it's not because of a car, there might be another reason a child wants to stop an activity their parents have invested countless dollars and hours on throughout the years. It might be for no other reason than he or she is tired of it. But it might also be for something tangible, like a car. And

42

that's something we parents at first just don't understand. That is, until we think back to our teenage years.

Besides wanting to skip baseball so he can work to buy a car, he is also thinking he'll sit on the varsity bench during baseball games this year and that he'd rather be honing his basketball skills than standing in the outfield shagging fly balls during batting practice. And shooting hoops can be scheduled around him working in the afternoon or evenings and on weekends.

I'm a big proponent that kids have the rest of their lives to drive and only a few years to be kids. But I also had my own car in high school and looking back on it, despite it being "just" the handed-down family station wagon, I can't imagine my life without it during those two years in high school.

So now he must sort out the plusses and minuses if he chooses not to play baseball this year.

The plusses are simple: He'll be able to work and afford his own car, and reap the benefits of having one, which in his mind already includes summer day trips to the beach and hanging out at the mall without dear old dad.

But one major minus is harder to accept: If he doesn't play baseball this year, his chances are slim to none he'll be selected next year if he decides to try out for the team. That's just the reality of high school sports.

He'll also have to increase the hours he is working to help pay for a car, which in turn actually will decrease his social time.

He's diligently researching the car issue. He also plans to talk to his coach and his manager at work before making his decision. He's scouring newspapers comparing car prices, figuring out how financing works, and has even decided he's going to do his senior project on the unfairness of insurance agencies toward teenage drivers.

This issue seems to have matured him light years compared to what any lecture of mine would have.

I guess my point is this: Every child at some point comes to a crossroads when a favorite activity might not be as important as it was at a different stage of life. As parents, it's up to us to listen, offer advice and guide. But we have to be careful not to judge and, if possible, not to be the ones to make the decision.

Deciding whether to participate in an extra-curricular activity is not a life-and-death choice, but sometimes as parents we lose sight of that, and often for selfish reasons. The situation can be used to teach a life lesson. In this case, it's a chance for a teenager to think through the circumstances of a life-altering decision. Just as importantly, he will have to accept the consequences.

It's a great lesson for him to learn. And important as parents we let him do so.

WHAT MAKES US RICH

A good friend is pondering one of the most difficult decisions he's faced as an adult as he tries to decide whether or not to leave a company he's been loyal to for over a decade for one that is aggressively recruiting him.

This friend — and no, this is not one of those stories where I am really the friend — has worked tirelessly as a salesman for one of the largest computer companies in the world. And when I mean tirelessly, he averages more than sixty hours a week and typically is up all night at least once during the week in order to properly prepare for a presentation.

He is paid handsomely, in money that is. From the stories I've heard it seems that he's underappreciated and those long hours are expected, not rewarded.

His new job would free his weekends up completely, which, with a wife and four kids, is certainly a plus. However, since he now would be overseeing three offices, the minus is losing the weekday flexibility of going to his kids' games or school activities in the afternoon. In other words, the perks of being a salesman and controlling his own schedule would now be gone.

Also gone would be the pressure to sell. His salary would almost double and not depend on commissions. "I'll make enough where my kids will think we're rich," he told me. And it was that statement that got me thinking about what really makes a family rich.

When I was younger I remember asking my parents if we were rich, and the answer I always got was the same: "We are very rich in many

45

ways." And while I didn't understand that response at the time, and took it as them ducking my question, I now know exactly what they meant.

My father was a dentist and my mother a teacher, and while we certainly were comfortable, his Volkswagen Beetle — before they were in style — parked in the professional building lot next to all the BMWs and other "rich" cars easily showed off to the world he did not fall into the stereotypical category of being a rich doctor.

His four-day workweek, combined with his daily two-hour lunch, ensured we were never spoiled rich, financially that is.

Both of my parents had and made time for all three of us children. Whether it was to pick up, drop off, or just be home so we could come and go around the neighborhood as we pleased, none of us ever felt abandoned by selfish, over-worked parents. We didn't live in a mansion, but the time spent under our roof was worth more than any house I've seen on "Cribs."

I also learned the difference between "want" and "need" from my parents. I always wanted a motorized scooter — called a moped back then — and swore to both parents I really needed one. They told me that one day I'd understand when I had kids of my own why we couldn't just go out and buy things, even if we could afford them.

At the time I didn't understand this, mainly because one of my best friends, whose mother was raising five kids on a part-time income, managed to somehow afford a moped. Since then I've realized that although he could afford the moped, his family never went on vacation and he was not able to finish college due to financial constraints. To his credit, he is ensuring his own three children see the world and go to college. And not one of them has a moped.

So of course, my parents were right … again.

I said, "No," when my oldest son wanted a go-kart. "But I need one," he pleaded. I'm convinced that somewhere my parents were smiling as he said it.

46

I'm not sure what decision my friend will make about his job, but the fact he's going through the process helped reaffirm to me that my average-paying job that allows me the flexibility to see my oldest son's varsity games and visit daycare on special days, has given me riches in ways money never could.

My parents always tried to explain this to me, usually when I selfishly wanted something I didn't really need. But like a lot of things, it took me to live it before realizing the life lesson I was learning.

It's one of many childhood lessons that have finally sunk in over the years, and one I'm convinced my boys will someday not only learn, but understand … albeit not from the cushioned seat of a motorized scooter.

MORNING ROUTINE

My morning could start at eight o'clock. I'd have plenty of time to shower, grab a quick bite to eat, head out the door and still arrive at work ahead of schedule.

But I have kids. So instead, my day starts three hours earlier and I don't get to work any sooner. In fact, sometimes I scoot in the back door hoping to be unnoticed.

The alarm blares, my wife heads into the shower and I unsuccessfully try to doze back to sleep, hoping that it's really Saturday and she's just confused, all the while listening for Riley's first peep of the morning.

While she feeds Riley, I head downstairs to make sure the automatic coffee machine really did start and help alleviate the dog's swollen bladder. I feed the dog and pour my first cup of pep and await the storm.

The wife and infant descend the stairs, the dog scratches at the door to come back in, and my five minutes of peace and quiet comes to an abrupt end. The day has now officially started.

I have to chase the high-schooler out of bed while dodging the toddler's walker and kissing my wife goodbye.

I feel like I've been up for hours despite being on my feet for less than one. The teenager is scarfing down blueberry pancakes while his little brother is trying to eat a toy three times bigger than his fist. My coffee is now cold and I still haven't showered. I haven't read the morning newspaper ... since the holiday vacation.

48

The bus has come and gone, Riley is tired of driving into things and the dog is nowhere to be found. And I'm still in my pajamas.

I put Riley on the floor with some toys and head into the shower. I peek out and make him laugh so he knows I'm still around. Of course, with every peek-a-boo, just a little bit more water ends up on the floor that now needs to be mopped up.

I get half-dressed before he's at a point when he has to be held. The pain from his three shots the day before and those two white things peeking through his gums are quickly decreasing his tolerance, along with my patience.

We head downstairs to eat and I call my wife to say "Have a great day" while stirring the oatmeal. Meanwhile, I get a text message from my oldest that there's a sports meeting after school and he will need a ride home.

All of a sudden, the stresses at work seem minor.

Riley finishes eating and I plop him down in front of "Mike and Mike" on ESPN2, pour some colored blocks on the floor for him to try and eat and turn on the computer to check emails.

Finally, it's time to head to daycare. I drop off Riley and he's happy as can be to be playing with other kids.

As I get back into the car and look at my watch, I realize that I've now been up for more than three hours. I have done absolutely nothing for myself and am lucky I remembered — after glancing down to double-check — to finish dressing before heading out the door.

I have to rush to work and still figure out how to get the teenager picked up from school. It's never easy. Being a parent never is.

As I breathe a sigh of relief during my drive to work, I think about the couples who wish they were parents. And parents who have lost a child far too soon.

And I decide I wouldn't trade my morning routine for anything in the world. Ever.

SPITTING OUT BIRTHDAY CANDLES

Riley turns two this weekend, but I won't even say it ... well, okay, I have to say it: The time has flown.

It seems like just yesterday we were loading him up in the car at the hospital for the first time. He wasn't squirming, didn't insist on watching "Barney," and my car seats were free of edible crumbs.

As I sit and write on this Saturday morning, he's on the floor talking — using four-word sentences — while putting together a puzzle that sometimes I struggle to complete. Or maybe I just don't have his patience.

The morning started off with a temper tantrum because he refused to be changed. This despite a wet diaper that I smelled the minute I entered his room in response to hearing, "I'm done sleeping, Daddy," at a time in the early morning when most people my age are just making their middle-of-the-night bathroom run.

We are trying to teach him there are consequences for misbehaving and like with most kids his age, the ultimate punishment is no television. A consequence he received last night.

So instead of a peaceful first hour to my weekend when he would normally sit quietly on the couch with his teddy and blanket watching the purple dinosaur — while I sip at my coffee and sift through the morning newspaper — he's ripping around the house, unloading every toy he owns out of the toy box, bugging his parents, and treating the dog as if he's part of a rodeo.

He's happier than a pig in you-know-what, and not just because he has a pile of it in his diaper.

50

Lesson learned? I'm not sure about him, but I learned I need to come up with another morning consequence. And I really do miss Barney.

Later the same day, we started planning for Riley's second birthday party. The first decision was an agreement to keep the gathering small and only invite two of his nearby cousins to help him ring in the "terrible twos."

Like most first-time parents, on his first birthday we packed the house with adult friends and relatives who mostly attended purely out of guilt, just like we've all done at one party or another.

The ones who had kids brought them, but because they were slightly older, the youngsters paid about as much attention to the birthday boy as the prom queen does to the class nerd.

We have some great pictures of Riley eating his first piece of cake with just his hands, crying when asked to pose for birthday pictures, and refusing to watch his parents open his birthday presents.

I'm actually not sure how we got so many pictures because from what I recall, after cleaning the cake off the wall and bandaging my paper cuts from the wrapping paper, I took him up to his crib for his daily afternoon siesta. There he napped peacefully until after the last guest departed.

So this year, we decided early on we were going to keep it small and invite just the two cousins and my parents. My in-laws were smart enough to skip town last week to their winter home.

Lo and behold, I'll be vacuuming shortly to prepare for an additional dozen adult guests. Instead of just having the planned meatball sandwiches and a box cake, we now have three main courses and four desserts.

Riley's godfather is driving three hours to watch him spew spit all over the birthday cake when it's time to blow out the candles; and I won't be surprised if my in-laws arrive by chartered plane before the day is over.

51

Lesson learned: We parents try not to make a big deal out of our children's special occasions, but sometimes we just can't help ourselves, and that's alright.

Truth be told, I'll enjoy my son's only celebration of turning two years old as much as anyone. And I'll even eat the cake after he spits at the candles to blow them out.

AS ARCHIE BUNKER WOULD SAY

On the morning of our departure for our annual beach vacation, Riley woke up in his worst mood of the summer. Every book and toy that was supposed to be getting packed was now his favorite. My wife seemed stressed out, most likely due to the fact that her to-do list was three pages and mine three items.

The car was packed to the roof. I honestly don't know what we'll do next year when we have to load a second port-a-crib and all that goes with it, including one more car seat. My wife has already volunteered to give up her space in the car to stay behind with the dog.

I remember when it was just my oldest and me. We traveled with one bag, a boogie board and suntan lotion. To borrow a phrase made famous by Archie and Edith Bunker: "Those were the days."

On Riley's first venture to the beach, he discovered that sand tastes awful but is fun to pile on your father, waves are powerful coming in and going out, and sand crabs don't like to be held.

He was mesmerized by the boats, but couldn't quite figure out the banners flying by. And he had no clue what I was pointing at while exclaiming, "Dolphin!"

It was just like my oldest on his first trip to the beach. It was because of him, after all, that my mother started this tradition more than a decade ago. Yes, the same first grandchild who this year opted out of our vacation to stay home and work.

Just like my oldest always did, Riley got up at the crack of dawn begging to go to the beach, which doesn't officially open until ten. I set the rule with my oldest that we couldn't go to the beach until the lifeguards were on duty. That particular rule, along with the one I made up about when you see the tractor driving by at night smoothing the sand it is the signal for all kids to get to bed, are two of my all-time best.

Normally with my oldest here, I make countless trips to the arcade, play miniature golf daily, and sneak in games of basketball and tennis. We always made a morning trip to the donut shop on our bikes and an evening walk to the ice cream parlor. But without him here, none of those father-son traditions are taking place, except in my mind.

I flew Riley's kite for him last night, just like I did for my oldest years ago.

As Riley naps and I sit here thinking back to those days when it was just my oldest and me here at the beach, I wonder where the time has gone. If he chooses to join us next year, he can drive here himself. He'll choose to sleep in over a donut and he'll only be interested in walking to get ice cream if there's a girl involved.

Next year, Riley will be a year older and braver. He'll be running into the waves instead of from them. He'll want me to bury him in the sand rather than the other way around. He'll understand the arcade and miniature golf, but still not the cost of doing either. He'll fly his own kite and be old enough to learn the myth about the lifeguards and tractor. Just like my oldest at that age.

I'll have one son driving a real car and be paying a quarter for another to ride in one at the arcade. One son will be heading to bed when the tractor goes by while the other one heads out on the town.

I'll try to get them both to play miniature golf with me. I'll never forget my oldest son's reaction when he made his first hole in one, and I can't wait to see Riley's. I'll probably let both of them beat me, just for old time's sake.

The reasons most people tell you they go on family vacations are to get away, relax, eat out and not have to do chores.

But the best reason is because family vacations are full of memories that although they pass, time can never take away.

MOWING PROVIDES LIFE LESSONS

Mowing the lawn is a thankless job that many of us started doing at a very young age. Back then we did it because we had to. Most likely in our home yard and didn't get paid. Or if we were lucky a neighbor was kind enough to pay us to do theirs.

My lawn cutting days started when I was five years old. No, my parents weren't irresponsible or foolish. I cut the grass using my sister's toy stroller. Don't laugh — well okay, go ahead — because it prepared me for when I finally cut the grass for real and I started learning many of life's most important lessons.

I used to cut my parents' lawn for free with that stroller. But my neighbor across the street was so impressed she paid me to do hers. That's right, paid me to cut her grass with a toy stroller. Of course, she paid me in candy, but at that age I spent any money I had on candy anyway, so she was just saving me a trip to the store.

Cutting the lawn with that stroller taught me a lot of things. I cut it as carefully as I do my own lawn now, making sure to overlap the next row with the wheel tracks just a little bit. I even ran the stroller over the sidewalk to mimic blowing the grass to the side. If they had made toy weed whackers like they do today I might have had to charge two candy bars.

As soon as I was old enough to use a real mower I got a few jobs mowing grass. Those lawn cutting jobs taught me much of the work ethic I would later use as a student and do today as an employee.

Lawn cutting is a job that you have to decide if and when it needs to be cut. People don't want to pay you if it isn't long enough to cut, but at the same time expect it to be done when warranted (but not during their family picnics or while the baby naps). So I learned how to evaluate and make timely decisions, which happens at my full-time job today.

Once the decision when to cut was made, I actually had to do it. If you've ever watched someone cut the lawn for the first time, you realize it's not as easy as it looks. If you aren't careful, you end up re-cutting in some places that have been cut and leaving high grass in other spots where it doesn't belong. So I learned how to stay focused while doing the job, despite many outdoor distractions. How many adults struggle with that at their jobs?

I often had to choose cutting the grass over playing baseball with my friends. People paid me to keep their lawn looking nice, so sometimes when the long grass needed my attention but so did my backyard team, I had to choose my job over a game. So cutting the grass taught me responsibility. In college, sometimes I had to choose studying over racquetball, and even today I often have to choose work over golf.

I had a few lawns to cut so I had to be organized. Between school and sports and other responsibilities, I had to juggle when I would get the lawns done. I had to watch the weather, pay attention to what time it got dark, and make sure my father wasn't using the mower. I learned how to budget my time and make sure to complete all of the things I had to get done (homework), wanted to get done (sports), and were responsible to get done (lawns).

Sounds like my life today. Just this morning I got my boys ready for daycare (have to get done), am going to bike at lunch (want to get done), and have several meetings at work (responsible to get done).

There are life lessons to be learned while pushing a mower, and I plan to make sure my boys do.

THE TEENAGER TRAVELS

One of my favorite movies growing up starred two comedians, Steve Martin and the late John Candy, and their adventures traveling across America trying to get home for the holidays. They traveled by plane, train and automobile and each adventure was wackier and funnier than the last.

My son has traveled on all three, but never alone. Next week he's heading to Florida with two neighborhood friends to visit a former cul-de-sac buddy. They'll drive to the airport, take a train through it and then board a plane. It will be just the three of them, all teenagers. Their parents and I will be nowhere in sight.

I've flown to almost every state in the country, so I know how easy and safe it is to fly. I've been seated with, in front of, and behind children traveling alone. They are treated like royalty, as they should be. Yet, I still worry.

I don't even think it's just the flight I'm worried about. It's the fact that he's going to be a plane ride away having a blast while I miss and worry about him like crazy. And my guess is, as with most teenagers, the only time my name will pop into his head is if he needs access to more money.

He wanted to go on this trip last year but sprung it on me at the last minute and so I didn't approve it. He was told by his mother and me if he wanted to go next year he'd have to plan ahead and save his money. I guess I was banking (no pun intended) on him not having his share of the fee. But he does, and next week he'll taxi down the runway without me.

He is headed to a lakefront house with a dock loaded with water toys. And did I mention they are within biking distance of the world's biggest playground, Disney World? It's a teenager's dream vacation.

His days will be spent running, swimming, laughing and having a grand old time. Mine will be spent worrying.

He'll sleep like a rock at night. Just not in his bed at our home.

He's in great hands down there. They just aren't mine.

It's a once in a lifetime opportunity for him. Just not with me.

I expected many questions from him about traveling alone with at least a slight show of nerves. I'm getting none. He's going into this trip with no fear. It reminds me of his first time on ice skates. He skated circles around me then, he's circling the globe without me now.

I guess I should be happy that he's excited to go, and in some ways proud that I've raised a child mature enough to take such a grownup trip. Maybe when he gets back safely I'll see it that way.

It seems like just yesterday he couldn't go anywhere without me loading him in the infant carrier and clicking him in. And then he graduated to the booster seat, the seat belt in the back, and then finally the front seat. Next year at this time he will be able to drive himself to the airport.

I guess it's time to let go, at least for a week. It will be the longest week of my life. But, I also realize, it is just the first of many long weeks ahead. Soon it might be summers, next will come semesters, and eventually he'll be away forever, coming home only to visit.

Each night this week that my oldest is gone, I'll go into Riley's room and kiss him goodnight twice. Once will be from me and the other for his big brother. And then I'll pop in the empty bedroom next door and stare at the empty bed. I'll close my eyes and trust he is safe and hope that when his head finally hits the pillow several states away, maybe, just maybe, he might miss me just a little.

It's tough letting go.

I DON'T WANT TO SIGN UP

The weather has teased you with hints of spring. Pitchers and catchers have reported to Florida and Arizona. The sporting goods stores are stocked with baseball gloves, tennis rackets and lacrosse sticks. Spring fever has set in.

You've been waiting since the day your child was born to sign him up for tee-ball, and the time has finally arrived. The only problem is he doesn't want to play.

He doesn't want to play soccer or lacrosse or try karate, either. He would rather use the racket you bought him to try and hit tennis balls over the house (I'd hide your golf balls). He only twirls the lacrosse stick you had him fitted for at age three to scoop debris out of the street gutters when it rains. And the baseball bat you bought him the day he was born is only swung at lightning bugs at dusk on those sticky summer nights.

Should you make him play?

I think it's very important for kids to be given opportunities to try different activities and sometimes that means forcing them to give it a shot. I'm not a proponent of making a child play a sport season after season if he doesn't want to, but I am okay with insisting he try it at least once. And this could hold true for any activity, not just sports.

In addition to developing motor skills and enhancing physical fitness, playing on youth sports teams builds social skills, often among a new and different group of friends. Kids need to learn how to get along with children from every background and of all abilities and attitudes, and sometimes they can't get that experience anywhere else.

60

The sport does not have to be baseball. One suggestion would be to tell your child that you want him involved in some sort of sports activity this spring, but he or she can pick what it will be. Nowadays, unlike when I was a kid, you can play just about any sport during any season.

One of the best sports for kids to see immediate success in is soccer. So if you are worried about your child keeping up with other kids, soccer might be the best sport to try. At any young age, basically if you can kick a ball any distance, follow a pack of kids to the ball, and enjoy the postgame snack, you can feel successful.

Sports aren't meant for every child. But every child should have the chance to give them a try.

A WEEK AT THE BEACH

I used to define a vacation as my wife and me packing one large gym bag filled with bathing suits, shorts and T-shirts, and getting on a plane that takes us to a place where the only thing we have to worry about is what all-inclusive drink to order next.

The only sand I would dig out of anyone's crevices is that which I managed to get on myself while laying horizontal all day, waiting for the above said drink to be refreshed.

But after spending a week at the beach "on vacation" with an infant and toddler, I started questioning whether it really was a vacation ... or just time off from work.

We packed our SUV for our five-day, four-night stay at the beach with enough stuff for what seemed like a month. And yet within an hour of our arrival my wife was at the grocery store buying more "essentials."

My two-year-old son touched the ocean for the first time that he can remember and quickly learned what undercurrent is and that the only thing worse than salt in your mouth is sand in your diaper. He also discovered that unlike the tub, Daddy can't make the water any warmer. He quickly realized the same thing about the pool; that, and the fact that chlorine tastes worse than sand.

Nap time was another adventure, as we used the excitement of a "big boy" bed — the reality was we couldn't fit a second pack-n-play in the car — as the incentive to take an unwanted rest. Fortunately, he was still naïve enough to believe his older cousins were doing the same, which made it a tad easier to put the ocean on hold for two hours each afternoon.

Unfortunately, his younger brother has a different nap schedule, so my rest time was virtually nonexistent. Just like the pity from his mother.

During my "vacation" I did manage to get a daily jog in each morning, which other than my time sitting in the bathroom with the newspaper was the only alone time I treated myself to the entire week.

But I guess it wouldn't be a family vacation if I wasn't around family. And boy was I. My parents, two siblings and their spouses, and five nieces and nephews created a mini family reunion. My brother's wife had six of her family members there as well. My wife truly is a saint.

Luckily my family is very easy going. I've heard horror stories of family vacations turning into year-long feuds. But with my family, nobody cares what you do during the day or who you do it with, as long as you take your kids with you. And there's always plenty of food and drink to share when Happy Hour finally arrives (which, this year, seemed to be earlier each day).

The cousins all played well together. The eldest, at ten, is still young enough to enjoy hide-and-seek, but old enough to let the others find her. And the younger kids all seemed to get along for the most part, or at least, when the going got tough, had the sense to evacuate to their own rooms where toys didn't have to be shared.

Nobody hit anyone with a miniature golf club, spilled ice cream on the boardwalk or threw sand in anyone's eyes. And none of them figured out that just one beach over there is a boardwalk filled with fun rides and games open well into the night.

My seventeen-year-old even ventured down for the day with a friend. But like other teenagers in this quaint resort, he quickly discovered that once you are off the beach and out of the pool, the quiet nightlife the rest of us enjoy about this town isn't quite as attractive for those with raging pimples and hormones.

My wife and I did manage to sneak away for one quick lunch on our own while my parents watched the boys. Needless to say, it was much better than my time spent reading the newspaper.

As we packed the car to leave — with somehow more stuff than when we arrived — we both decided that as much fun as our first few vacations alone were without kids and relatives, there really isn't anything better than vacationing with family.

At least that's what I told myself while checking out and paying the bill.

A VALUABLE SERMON

The Christians will tell you Sundays are for church. My oldest son says it's a day to sleep … and sleep … and sleep.

If he could talk, my dog would tell you it's just another day to eat and lay around, like every other day that ends in the letter "y."

I'm sitting here on a Sunday morning having been up for two hours with my ten-week-old son.

I've read and sorted the paper for my wife.

I've fed the dog and myself and had two cups of coffee.

I've done the dishes, straightened up a little bit, paid the bills, packed my gym bag, and now await my wife to arise so I can head to the gym.

Is my wife lazy? Actually, quite the opposite. She was up four times feeding the little guy in the middle of the night. I managed to sleep through three of them and during the fourth one I rolled over so I could count that as being awake. So at the crack of dawn when he was ready to stare wide-eyed and chat like only a ten week-old can, despite her telling me to just stay in bed and she'd go downstairs, I volunteered to get up and shoot the breeze with him.

Of course, we weren't downstairs more than thirty minutes into the morning sports report and he was fast asleep. My wife would say sports news puts most people to sleep, but regardless, I now have the next hour or so to myself to write about this unexpected and unsolicited Sunday quality time.

He'll never remember it, I'll never forget it. I wonder how many other dads get up with the kids and let mom sleep.

My guess is every dad does it at some point during the year, probably Mother's Day or maybe on her birthday. I imagine on those days maybe mom's sleep is interrupted with that famous breakfast in bed from the kids that she pretends to appreciate when truth be told she would have much rather had just one more hour of shuteye and two less pieces of burnt toast.

I try to let my wife sleep on Sunday mornings whenever I can.

Yes, I do it partly for her sake. It gives her a chance to catch up on sleep that she doesn't get during the week, when, despite being up in the middle of the night feeding as I'm dreaming, she still has to get up when the baby does in the morning because I head off to work.

But I also do it for me. Sunday morning is the one time during the week when I don't have to rush around to get ready for work or take our oldest son to school or get him to a Saturday morning practice. It's the one morning when the trash trucks aren't running, the school parking lot across the street isn't buzzing with laughter, and for some reason the dogs on either side of our house aren't howling at anything that moves.

It gives me a chance to spend uninterrupted time with my baby son chatting away. I talk to him about whatever I'm thinking and he listens, or at least pretends to be focused on my words. He doesn't talk back and right now at this age, rarely gives any indication that he cares at all.

He stares at me out of the corner of his eyes, cooing once in a while, kicking his feet occasionally and of course making sounds to remind me he'll need a diaper change shortly.

He tugs at my finger, wails his arms, and I'm convinced tries to see the sports ticker running across the screen.

He turns his head toward my chest and opens his mouth searching for something that only mom can give him, but then seems content with another binky plugged into his mouth for temporary satisfaction. All the while I chat away. Of course, the dog thinks I'm crazy, as even he seems smart enough to realize it's a one-way conversation.

Eventually my wife will come downstairs and thank me and tell me I'm a wonderful husband for letting her sleep a little longer and using the time to do a few things around the house to make her morning routine a little bit easier.

Little does she know, I'm the one who should be saying, "Thanks for the time."

MAKING THE PARTY 'A'-LIST

My youngest son was christened last weekend. And before he even had the chance to cry out, "Holy you-know-what," as water was being dumped over him and some awful-smelling oil was smeared on his head, there was what I call a tier-club controversy.

There are basically four tiers of friends in most marital situations. Tier One consists of immediate family including grandparents and our siblings and their families. Extended family of aunts, uncles and cousins make up Tier Two. Your closest friends you often treat like family are Tier Three. That leaves work colleagues and that second level of friends whose viewing you'd probably attend but whose wedding you didn't, and they fall into the Tier Four category.

Our immediate family is large on both sides. Our parents are alive and we each have two siblings with spouses and multiple nieces and nephews. So even just inviting members from the Tier One club means that we're cooking, cleaning and paying for almost thirty people.

So we've decided that for certain occasions — especially the ones when the guest of honor won't even remember who was in attendance like baptisms and early birthday parties — we are only going to invite Tier One club members. And as an aside, there are no membership dues to any of these clubs because let's face it, other than the grandparents, nobody would pay to be part of them.

Tier Two club members for the most part could care less if they are invited to these events. Sure, they'd come if invited, but have never once questioned when they weren't.

Tier Three members are a different story. That is, at least the female members of them.

Most male members of the Tier Three club prefer not to be invited to these affairs. It's one less event to dress up for, one less gift to buy, and three more hours to manicure the lawn, take a nap in between innings or just watch the grass grow so it needs to be mowed the next time an excuse to get out of a gathering is needed.

But as my wife quickly pointed out as we were developing the guest list, women are funny when it comes to things like this.

And so, sure enough, we got a call from a female member of the Tier Three club questioning why her family wasn't invited to the christening.

She pointed out that we were invited to both of her kids' baptisms at a fancy restaurant and that they always invite us to family functions. So shouldn't that mean we have to reciprocate?

If the guest of honor had his way, his baptism day would have included his normal nursing, nurturing, napping and a diaper change or two mixed in somewhere. And the only water dumped on him would have been at tubby time ... and not directly on his head (seriously, does it matter if the water is poured on his belly instead?). And there would have been no guests invited to watch any of this, except his mother, of course.

But since he's not in charge — except in the middle of the night — we decided to celebrate his baptism with just our Tier One club members and his godparents.

My wife tactfully explained to her friend that we have several people in our Tier Three club, so as soon as we dip into that membership list, our somewhat small family gathering becomes a party that causes even our neighbors to think they must have lost the invitation.

It took some time, but to her credit, the disgruntled friend understood. But my guess is if she and her husband have any more kids, I will have time both to watch the grass grow and cut it on the day of the baptism.

I'm not a party-pooper. In fact, I'm the first to say the more the merrier. I've been the recipient of several glares from my wife at football tailgates when I've invited practically strangers. I would have been all for a large baptism party except for the fact that, as my wife reminded me during the discussion, the credit card bill would eventually arrive and I'd be mortified how much it cost me to have people eat, drink and be merry while the guest of honor napped.

So for now, our family tradition of inviting only Tier One club members to certain functions will stay intact. Fortunately, most people from all four tiers understand.

And the men of those clubs couldn't be happier.

THE CAR RIDE HOME

How many of your kids wish like heck they could call a taxi after a ball game? Or any other activity where we parents feel free to give advice.

I know my oldest son would have quite a few times and offered to pay for it himself.

I learned very early in my parent-coach role that the last thing he ever wanted to talk about on the way home from his game was the game itself. It didn't matter whether he played well or poorly, won or lost. He didn't want to hear my best postgame speech in the car.

That didn't change when I became a parent in the bleachers.

I once went on for five minutes about a few game details (actually, maybe more than a few) that I would have liked to see him do better. I followed my five-minute barrage of hints and ideas with, "You know I'm only trying to help, right?"

He responded, "Yes, but do we really need to discuss it now? The game is over, let it rest." And you know what? He was right. And by the way, he was seven. I was thirty-two. Who says kids aren't smart?

So I swore right then and there that I would never talk about a game or practice on the car ride home again. And I haven't. All I say is, "Good game, you played well." But it sure

71

hasn't been easy and on more than one occasion I suggested he ride home with his mother.

I don't mean we never talk about the game. In fact, we always did and still do, even now after his high school games. We just do it when he's ready and we talk about the things he wants to discuss. I make a point to just listen. Even if I don't agree with his analysis, I don't say anything unless he asks me my opinion and then I do tell him my thoughts, whether I think he'll like it or not. But I also tell him it is just that, my opinion, and he can disagree if he wants and his coach and other parents might also.

What have I learned? That like most adults, kids want to talk when they are ready and prefer to be supported and listened to rather than lectured and criticized. And you know what? Typically, when I just wait for him to want to talk, I get to make the points I wanted to make anyway, just in a very non-threatening manner that he is much more responsive to.

Think about your last car ride home from a game. Was it spent talking about all the things that he could have done better? Or about what your child wanted to talk about? My guess is the former. After the next game, try the latter.

FINDING THAT COMMON BOND

My father collects antiques. I collect Bobbleheads.

My father explores gravesites in his pursuit of genealogical history. I tour stadiums for the fun of it.

My father's lawn is impeccable. Mine is filled with pretty yellow flowers.

My father is the church organist. I begged out of piano lessons as a child.

We looked just alike as kids and my mother and wife swear we share many of the same personality traits including stubbornness (no I'm not) and thinking we are always right (we are). So I'm definitely his child. But like most fathers and sons, I don't have everything in common with dear old Dad. And neither does my brother.

My brother is an accountant, I work for a nonprofit and my father is a retired dentist.

I'm an avid sports fan, my brother an average one and my father not at all.

My brother's Super Bowl is election night, my father follows politics but not passionately, and I still can't decide if I'm a republican or democrat, and quite frankly don't really care.

My brother and father both collect antiques. Their houses are full of them. They often bid against each other online for this thing called two-panel glass. They both have an uncanny ability to clutter a house with dust-collecting, "don't-touch" items that could easily be traded in for season

73

tickets with plenty of money left over for hotdogs and beer. The only two-panel bowl my father gave me is used to store the remotes.

Dad and I, we love to write. As you might expect, we each write about different subjects. He has authored a book about a significant historical figure while mine was about coaching kids. He writes a quarterly fact-filled column in his historical society's newsletter. My weekly newspaper columns are off-the-cuff thoughts about parenting and youth sports.

As his sons, the most important thing is not how much we have in common with our father, but just the fact that we each enjoy something in common with him. Father's Day is a time when sons should make sure they've found something in common with their dads. It might be a love of sports, museums or antiques. Or as in my case, it might be something much less tangible ... and much cheaper than antiquing.

Too often fathers and kids think that if it can't be visited with an admission ticket, purchased with a credit card or placed on a shelf, it can't be considered something in common. And nothing could be further from the truth.

I've found that connection with Dad. I enjoy reading what he writes and vice versa. It doesn't even matter if the subject isn't of interest to either of us because it's more the fact that someone we love and respect has created a work worth reading. We also share other newspaper clippings, magazine articles and websites that we know will be of interest to the other.

When my brother visits he gets to see the latest dust-filled two-panel thingamajig. When I visit I'm usually handed a newspaper clipping he knows I'll enjoy reading.

My father has played a vital role in my life from the very beginning. He worked hard so I could get a higher education and was the main person who convinced me that I should go to college for what I wanted to do, not what would pay me the most.

He went to college to be a dentist. I went to be a teacher. Something tells me if we each had to do it over again, we might both major in journalism. Instead it has become a hobby we share. For two people who don't have many mutual interests on paper, we certainly have found a common link on just that ... paper.

At an awards ceremony a few years ago my father was recognized for his contributions to the community through his writing. In his congratulations card I wrote: "One of the greatest gifts you've ever given me is the opportunity to admire you."

Fortunately, he has passed onto me another gift - the passion and enjoyment of expressing myself in writing.

It's a gift that can't be wrapped, but can still be shared between us ... just father and son.

A FRAMABLE GIFT

Last year on Father's Day I penned a column about how the greatest gift a son could give his father is to find something in common with him, like I had with my father through our love of writing.

And then on the actual day itself my son presented me with his gift. It was a frame, and in it, a copy of his own column he wrote for me. He had not had the chance to read the column I wrote for my dad so it was purely coincidental how similar they were.

When I was three years old, my dad and I used to play floor hockey in the basement every night. I would beat him every time even if he let me win, which was an honor in itself. My dad and I also played basketball, baseball and football every night. I used to be amazed how far he could hit the ball, how high he could jump, and how long he could throw a perfect spiral. These memories allowed me to love sports and share that love with my dad.

As I grew up my dad coached my teams and I matured into an athlete as his player and son. I always loved having him as a coach because we could always have a long talk in the car on the way home about the game and the upcoming opponents. My dad also taught me good sportsmanship and how to be a part of a team. Even if I was the best player on the team and would just rather play alone, he taught me the importance of teammates. These aspects of sports taught me to respect the game along with loving it.

My dad taught me how to play every sport I know and continue to play today. Even if he now shies away from my slap shot, can't dominate me on the boards in one-on-one, and can't cover me in touch football, he knows he is the reason that I love sports and enjoy loving them with him. He continues to teach and coach me as a high school athlete. I think that's all an athlete and son can ask for.

Dad ... Happy Father's Day!

I always knew how much our love of sports meant to me, but it wasn't until that day that I understood just what it meant to him.

My days of coaching him on the fields and courts ended last summer. They were times I'll never forget. What I'm proudest of is that through the good and bad, win or lose, we were always father and son before coach and athlete.

Now I spend my time as his number one fan. A few weeks ago I sat in right field and watched him launch his first-ever home run over the right field fence. I can't remember a moment in my life as a sports fan when either of us was happier.

We play one-on-one hoops in the driveway three nights a week. I no longer have to let him win. In fact, I struggle to take one of our three games each night. Since I'm the one who taught him how to shoot a jumper, I'm sort of proud that I lose (at least that's what I tell myself).

Our relationship as coach-athlete is over, my days of being his biggest fan are coming to a close, and my knees will only be able to take so many more driveway games. But being sports fans is something that time and age can't take away from us.

When he was four years old I convinced him he should root for the New York Jets and Philadelphia Phillies. Fortunately, he hasn't held the former against me.

We go to several college and professional games a year, watch others on television, and when we can't be together for whatever reason, technology keeps us in constant contact during games that are important to us.

No matter what he does for a living, where he ends up settling, or what his family situation becomes, even if we aren't sitting in the stands together, I know we'll keep in touch during the big games.

Sports aren't for everyone, but as his letter reads, it's always been something special to us. To borrow his phrase: It's something I enjoy loving with him.

LESS THAN PERFECT TIMING

How does the old saying go? Sometimes, the best laid plans ...

Everything in my wife's and my life together so far has been timed perfectly.

We met at a perfect time in each of our professional and personal lives. She had just put the final touches on a big project for her job as a teacher that took eight months to complete. I was winding down coaching two youth sports. The months leading up to when we met were filled with other commitments, and a relationship was the last thing for which either of us would have had time.

But one month later, when we finally did meet, we both had free time.

It was a whirlwind courtship after meeting online. During those first few months, we realized all the places we have both been at different times, all the chances we could have met but didn't, and all the friends and professional acquaintances we had in common. But for some reason, it just wasn't time to meet before we did. But finally, when we did meet, the timing was perfect.

The ring arrived one week ahead of schedule and I proposed just three days before her last day of school so that she could share the good news with her friends and colleagues. Once again, timing was everything. If the ring doesn't arrive early, the news she's been waiting to share all her life would be old news when school started up again in September.

We decided to wed just before Christmas that same year. The timing would be perfect to allow us to honeymoon and get back for the

79

holidays and have the next two weeks off thanks to our job schedules. It seemed too good to be true. The timing couldn't have been better. We had a summer to plan and three weeks to begin our life together in December.

And then Riley came along, born within a week of when we had hoped to allow for maximum time at home before going to daycare the following school year.

He was born just in time to meet his great-grandmother before her passing and my longtime pet dog before hers. One month later, he would have missed both chances.

Our move to the new house happened when Riley was the perfect stage to pack up a house - the immobile stage.

So far, so good. Our timing couldn't have been better from start to finish. Until now, that is.

You see, our plan was to have another baby next May. With my wife having fewer sick days to use, the birth ideally had to happen closer to the end of the school year. And so, of course, we assumed it would. After all, everything else since we met had been timed perfectly.

Well, as I mentioned, that is until now. The other day my wife emerged from the bathroom with her pregnancy test in tow and a look of concern on her face. There was no "iffy" result. Without a doubt, Riley is going to be a big brother.

My wife is eight weeks into her pregnancy, and if you do the math, no matter how you add it up, the baby won't be born in May. Rather it will be sometime between Thanksgiving and Christmas of this year. The fact we can write him or her off our taxes is the only well-timed part of this.

My wife immediately panicked. "We can't have a baby then. What are we going to do?" she asked. "Looks like we'll be having a baby in December," I brilliantly replied. Fortunately, the yet-to-be born child couldn't count the number of fingers Mommy was holding up, or see which one.

The news was completely unexpected, but we quickly came to our senses and realized that having a baby isn't automatic, no matter when you hope and try to time it. We have several friends who have been trying and still are, and would gladly take a mistimed pregnancy over a perfectly timed one in a heartbeat.

So we took a deep breath, embraced, smiled at each other and felt a tug on our legs. It was Riley. He looked up at us and smiled.

I think somehow he knew he was going to be a big brother.

He seemed to be very happy about it. Almost as happy as his parents.

BEST JELLY DONUT EVER

I heard it over and over a thousand times when I first became a dad fifteen years ago. People would all say: "The time flies by, enjoy every second of it." I always agreed with a nod of the head and a "yeah, right" to myself, but never imagined it to be true. Take it from me, it is.

Having just witnessed the birth of my second child and then watched my fifteen-year-old son hold his sibling in between studying for high school honors classes made me think, "Wow, time did fly by."

I still remember when that teenager first rolled over, crawled, walked and talked. He walked when he was one, talked when he was two, was potty-trained at three, got his first set of golf clubs at four, and we took the training wheels off at five. He made it simple to remember those major milestones.

I survived "Barney," the "Rugrats" and the "Power Rangers." I now suffer through MTV and have to actually pay attention to the themes in the sitcoms he watches.

I still remember times that he cried, others when he laughed, and some when he wasn't sure what emotion to show. Our favorite spots were the marina docks when he was a toddler, the doughnut shop on Saturday mornings once he started school, and any type of sporting event ever since.

We were inseparable and it seemed there was nothing he liked more than doing anything and everything with me. Now he seems to enjoy spending time with his friends more than dear old Dad. I guess he's normal, though, looking at how his other friends spend their time and thinking back to myself at that age. Best friends or Dad? It was an easy decision back then for me (sorry, Dad). And an easy decision today for him (that's okay, son, I understand, at least most of the time).

Just today he called to tell me he got a perfect report card and it was like a flashback in time. He was proud of himself and even prouder to tell me. I still remember the first perfect paper he brought home in grade school. He was just as proud of that finger-painted picture back then as he was of his honors-class grades today. And so was I, and am I.

Last week I was late driving him to the bus stop and he missed it. And so I had to drive him to school and on our way we decided to stop at the doughnut shop since he'd be early. Jelly donuts and conversation, just like old times.

I can't wait for the first person to tell me to "enjoy every second" of this newest edition to our family because "time will fly." Unlike most new fathers when asked that question, I'll be able to answer it from experience with a down-to-earth, honest, "Don't worry, I know time flies. It already did."

Fortunately, the memories of raising my son are something that nobody can take away. Gone are our weekly trips to the marina and the doughnut shop. His golf clubs are nicer than mine and his two-wheeler will soon be replaced with four wheels. But in my mind I still see that smile whenever he saw a big boat on the docks and I will always remember the sound of his voice when he ordered and paid for that first jelly doughnut all by himself. Time can never take that away.

I should be late to the bus stop more often.

SPECTATING AT GAMES

This week I give out my award for the best spectator ever. I'll call him Wayne. Wayne spends his spare time following his grandchildren's youth sports teams. It really doesn't matter where they play or what the sport, he seems to show up at just about everything.

For a recent baseball tournament he drove two hours to watch his grandson play in one game. And then drove two hours home.

Wayne arrived shortly after the first pitch with his chair in tow. He set up "camp" away from all the spectators, but with a perfect view of the field. And then to my surprise he pulled out a book. I couldn't believe my eyes. A four-hour round-trip drive and he was going to read a book. He looked up whenever he heard the crack of the bat.

In between one inning his grandson was near him, warming up the left fielder and that caused him to look up. Most parents or grandparents would have some sort of baseball advice, especially since his grandson had just struck out. Not Wayne. His only words: "I have a great book for you to read!"

I turned to another parent and said, "Wayne has it all figured out, doesn't he?" The rest of us are stressing out over watching teenagers play baseball and his only care in the world this day is making sure his grandson realizes there are more important things in life than baseball.

And so you might ask yourself, "Why drive four hours to read a book?"

Well, believe it or not, after the game Wayne could recall just about every critical play, which is more than I can say, thanks to my gift for spectator gab. Every player he passed after the game was congratulated for something that specifically happened during the game. Once again I thought to myself that Wayne has it all figured out.

As I listened to the other parents barking at the umpires or their own kids, I had to sit and wonder that if all of us took a chapter out of Wayne's book, the youth sports world would be a better place.

Wayne drove two hours to the game, watched his grandson bat once and have zero attempts in the field. Our team got creamed in less than two hours. Wayne closed his book, folded up his chair, sent along a few "nice jobs" and drove two hours home with a smile on his face. In his mind, time perfectly spent.

All of us dads and moms could learn from Wayne. Because Wayne has it figured out.

THE BEACH BOYS

I had been looking forward to our annual beach vacation with my entire extended family for weeks, realizing that this year with two mobile little boys, the amount of rest we'd get would be limited but the memories made priceless. And finally the time had come.

Prior to departure, my only instruction from my wife during the packing period was to lay out the clothes I wanted and she would take care of everything else. I figured there was no way she would remember everything I needed. Within five minutes of our arrival at our rented ocean-front condominium I suggested that I should have brought my binoculars. Sure enough, my wife packed them. I would have never found them at home, let alone remember to pack them. There was not one thing the entire week I needed and didn't have. Clearly, that's why I'm relegated to packing the car, and not packing for the trip. She is amazing.

Day 1: Riley (three years old) and Tyler (eighteen months) couldn't wait to get to the ocean and join their cousins. Riley, with fond memories from last year, took to the water with an air of confidence that was almost scary. Tyler was a bit more timid, which wasn't surprising considering he spent last year's entire trip sitting on a blanket, most likely thinking: "They pay all this money for me to sit on a blanket under an umbrella. This is what I do at home in the backyard." However, by the end of the morning session he had become quite comfortable sitting in a blowup pool where the water meets the beach, probably thinking: "They pay all this money for me to sit in a blowup pool? This is what I do at home in the backyard."

Day 2: Both boys were up earlier than usual, clearly not aware that vacations are meant for sleeping in. Fortunately, they believed us when we told them that they couldn't go in the ocean until the lifeguards were on duty and that all those other kids in the water would probably have to go to timeout. Once on the beach, Riley discovered the fun of riding a boogie board. All he needed was me to get him started when the wave broke just right and off he went. Unfortunately, this meant I had to get wet above my ankles. He was in heaven. Meanwhile, clearly overtired from waking up too early, Tyler decided his mother should carry him around on her hip all morning. She was in hell … a very hot, sticky, sandy and expensive hell.

Day 3: Both boys were up an hour earlier than the previous morning when they were up too early. Tyler had sunscreen rubbed into his eyes before we even left the condo, and then tried rubbing it out with his sandy hands the second his feet touched the beach. We took our first trip to the arcade in the afternoon where we spent ten dollars on each boy to earn enough tickets for a fifty-cent trinket.

Day 4: The overnight before our last full day we brilliantly split the boys up for sleeping thinking maybe they'd sleep in until the sun was at least almost up. Riley was in his own room and Tyler in with us in a port-a-crib. They both set a new all-time record for waking up early. Tyler loved the beach today, the sand part that is. He sat and poured sand into his dump truck for over an hour, most likely thinking to himself: "They pay all this money for me to play in this big sandbox. This is what I do at home in the backyard." Oh, and after three days we finally figured out exactly what we needed to take to the beach, leaving behind the two chairs neither of us had unfolded yet.

Day 5: Somehow without buying a single souvenir — I considered the nightly ice cream cones a souvenir — we managed to leave the resort area with more stuff than when we arrived. The one exception was Tyler's shoe, which was dropped into the giraffe pen at the zoo. As soon as we arrived home, both boys sprinted for the backyard, where they spent the afternoon wading in the blowup pool and playing in the sandbox. It was then that my wife and I finally were able to sit in our beach chairs on the patio while we watched them splash around and make sand castles, me thinking, "We spent all that money … ."

MY MAN-CATION

It was the best of times. It was the worst of times.

Truth be told, there were no worst of times on my "man-cation." Three buddies and I ventured to Fenway Park and Yankee Stadium for back-to-back games at two of the most famous sports venues in the world.

Each of us left a wife and our children behind, which somehow made the trip even ... what's the word I'm looking for ... okay, better!

I have to be honest that once in a while it's nice to put the mature adult in you aside. At our ages, this means enjoying a few adult beverages at the game without having to escort anyone to the bathroom or stand in line for ice cream.

We went with the thinking that "What goes on in Boston stays in Boston." Fortunately, for our families at home, and even more so for us, nothing happened that couldn't be repeated at the dinner table the first night home. That's also the reality of trying to relive your early twenties in your forties.

We drove up to Boston in my minivan, which clearly was an indicator of exactly what phase of life each of us is in. That and the fact that the thought of opening a sudsy beverage while in the car never even entered our minds. Instead the chatter during the ride encompassed everything from one daughter throwing her poop around her bedroom to the latest sports headlines, along with work topics and retirement dreams mixed in. Not exactly the conversations we had while taking college road trips.

And did I mention our aging bladders caused more stops than when we travel with our wives and kids.

Once we arrived at the hotel we somehow managed to sneak a cooler filled with adult beverages onto the pool deck. Actually, the story just sounds cool if I say we sneaked it on, when the reality is we didn't know there was a rule against it and I very intelligently just strode through the crowd wondering why I was getting funny glares. I assumed it was people gawking at my farmer's tan. Well, actually, maybe they were doing that, too.

We lasted less than an hour before we decided it might be a good idea to get out of the sun and head back to the rooms for a quick rest — I remember making fun of my grandparents for needing an afternoon nap — before our night out on the town. A train ride later we stood in line at a restaurant outside the ballpark for what seemed like an eternity to buy an over-priced beer while waiting over an hour for a seat just to eat. Something tells me back in college we would have settled for a half-cooked stadium hot dog and had so many beers in us by that point the price would have been irrelevant.

Once in the stadium not one of us bought a beer — "I'm not spending that kind of money on a beer!" — but each of us did have a plastic helmet filled with ice cream. And although official statistics are not kept, something, or someone, like the person we kept bothering to get out of our seats, tells me we might have shattered the record for trips to the bathroom thanks to those aforementioned aging bladders.

After the game we stopped at a bar and played beer pong. Okay, truth be told, we played video golf and whined about how tired we all were. We were tucked in bed well before last call (but all called home first).

The next day on our final leg of our journey, we sat in our seats for just one sun-drenched hot inning at Yankee Stadium before deciding our time would be better spent in the air-conditioned stadium bar, where we ordered and complained about over-priced food and not one of us was in the mood for a real drink.

The talk on the way home was how much each of us missed our kids, while none of us was manly enough to admit we also missed our wives.

There wasn't one more mention of sports or beer, but we did all agree we should take this "man-cation" annually ... and next time take our wives and kids.

Then it truly will be the best of times.

MRS. FIXIT

Spring chores are just around the corner. Mr. Fixit I'm not. I never had that gene and never will. In fact, if you look back on my family tree, I don't think that gene ever made the boat ride over to America. My father used to tell me by not being handy he was providing employment for others. I've provided plenty of that.

My wife, however, is different. She is the Mrs. Fixit in our house and is called on more than I am to do the routine house repairs. That would be me doing the calling. I can cut the grass, take out the trash and even unclog the toilet. I even swear I could figure out the new front-loading washer if given the chance (that would be if, not when). But if it involves more than a hammer or duct tape, my wife gets the nod. And actually, if the hammering or taping requires accuracy, she gets that job, too.

For example, a few months ago I heard a loud bang upstairs in one of the bedrooms as I was intently watching a football game. Before I could even react (i.e. the next commercial), my wife yelled down that she was fine and not to worry. Five minutes later, she came down and I asked what happened. Her response: "The closet track broke and the door fell off, punched a hole in the wall and banged against the dresser. It's already fixed."

Whew!

Some men would probably scoff at me for letting my wife do all the major household repairs. I don't think this makes me a bad or incompetent husband, just a husband bad at fixing things. But at least I admit it and am not embarrassed to let my wife wear the tool belt in our family. My guess is households spend thousands of dollars a year paying handymen following attempted repairs by "the man of the house" who is too macho to let his wife fix things.

Not me. "Go to it, honey. Let me know if I can get you something to drink."

My guess is my oldest son will have to do the same, since he certainly isn't learning these things from me and seems more interested in watching sports and texting his friends than learning from his stepmother how to put a door back on track and spackle a hole in the wall. I have taught him the art of ripping a piece of duct tape off the roll and how to handle the stringy stuff when you don't tear it just right (wad it up, throw it away and tear off another piece). I'm waiting until he turns sixteen to introduce the hammer. Spackling will have to wait until adulthood.

Does this make me a bad dad? No, just a dad bad at fixing things. But to be honest, I think it's just as important to teach him not to be ashamed to let a woman do a "man's job" than it is to have him watch me wreck the house one fixit job at a time. And by watching me dust, vacuum and do other household chores, it has enabled me to demonstrate how to vacuum without running over the cord (most of the time) and dust around the trophies and Bobbleheads on his shelf, all while being entertained by fifty heads bobbling at once. This amuses me to no end. My wife, not so much when she dusts.

It also is good for him to see me cook and help fold the laundry (front loader or not, I can do that). He now knows why for years when he put his socks in the laundry inside out, he got them back inside out. His wife will thank me one day. He has also mastered microwave cooking, except for popcorn, and I don't think anyone can master that.

What I'm trying to teach him is what my parents always stressed to me. There no longer are "women's chores" and "men's chores," just chores that need to be done. And finished right, the first time.

93

Does this make me a slacker dad or husband? Nah. After all, I'm not trying to get out of doing chores to watch a game; but it is a great excuse. Rather, I'm trying to avoid wrecking the house and instead letting the person who fixes things the best in my house repair mishaps — often mine — correctly the first time.

I actually think it makes me a man with a newly discovered gene. Call it whatever you want, but I hope one day my son will appreciate this gene I'm passing on to him.

Along with the duct tape and hammer, every man should carry this gene on his tool belt.

CONVERSING WITH YOUR KIDS

How many of us have had this conversation with one of our teenagers in the car after a long day at school:

Parent: "How was school today?"

Child: "Fine."

Parent: "What did you do?"

Child: "Nothing."

End of conversation.

I usually reply that if he isn't doing anything in school, it's a good thing I'm not paying for him to attend (if I told him I was paying public school taxes, he'd ask to opt out and save me the money).

As a parent like me, you probably get frustrated that your teenager doesn't want to share all of his or her escapades from the school day. When they were in elementary school, you got to hear about every last detail in long, drawn-out, theatrical fashion. Now you're lucky if you hear anything. There are probably some things you really need to know, some you want to know, and, more than likely, many you are better off not knowing at all.

I need to know his latest grades and when the next project is due, but would prefer not to hear about who got the wedgie in the locker room. I'd love to know who his latest crush is on, but don't need to know what antics took place in the cafeteria or at recess.

I found myself getting more and more aggravated that my son would rather listen to the radio or play on electronics during the drive home from school instead of chatting with dear old dad about life's ups and downs. But then I started thinking about it on my quiet ride home from work.

After my long day on the job, I get in the car and have a twenty-minute commute home. There is nobody to talk to and nobody to listen to. And to be honest, when I think about it, I enjoy every second of that twenty minutes. The last thing I would want to do is have to leave work and immediately talk about everything I did for the past eight hours. My guess is if you think about it, you are the same way. So why would our almost-adult children be any different?

By the time I've enjoyed that tranquility of my commute and arrive home, shower and sit down to dinner, I'll talk about anything and everything. Just ask my wife. So I tried this strategy with my son, and you know what, it worked. After an almost-silent ride home, dinnertime was nonstop chatter from him. And it wasn't a one-night occurrence.

Communicating with our children is one of the most important roles we have as parents. But like adults, kids will have times when they do and don't want to talk. The key is taking advantage of the times they do and listening to what they have to say, no matter what we'd rather talk about or be doing.

Wedgies aside, the best conversation you can have with your children is any conversation they are willing to have with you.

WHEN TO START PLAYING SPORTS

I was at a children's birthday party last weekend and the topic of how young is too young to start playing sports came up.

I just sat back and listened to the various opinions. One grandmother offered to pay for her granddaughter to play youth sports. The mother of that daughter, a former Division I field hockey player, is adamantly against her daughter playing any organized sport until she is at least five years old.

One mom started her son in soccer at the age of four while another has decided six is a good age. A dad, who is a former high school basketball coach, is debating whether his four-year-old son is ready.

Other mothers and fathers chimed in, and just when I thought I had lost the chance to give my opinion, my wife spoke up: "Jon, you write about youth sports. What do you think?"

I actually think it depends on a number of things when determining what age a child should start playing sports. First and foremost is the interest of the child. If he or she has no interest whatsoever, it's probably too early to start.

The second is the physical and emotional maturity of the child. If the child is scared to death of any physical contact, he or she won't be interested in being part of a soccer scrum. If his feelings get hurt every time someone takes a toy from him, imagine his or her reaction the first time a child "steals" the ball.

When my middle son was four years old, he was more than ready to start playing soccer and since then has successfully played tee-ball and flag football. I can't imagine my youngest son, who just turned four, playing anything organized right now. And that's another thing to remember, just like all developmental stages, siblings will be ready at different times.

I also think one factor often overlooked by parents when trying to make this decision is how the family will be affected by a child playing an organized sport at such a young age.

If bedtime is at seven — to allow for not only a good night sleep but also "down time" for mom and dad — and practice is twice a week until seven, that means the family routine is going to be upset two of the four school and work nights.

If there is more than one child at home, what happens to the non-practicing siblings the night of practice? Will a younger sibling be dragged out of the house when she would normally be in bed? Will an older sibling's grades suffer because he is sitting in a car at a practice instead of at the kitchen table getting assignments done?

All of these things must be taken into consideration.

I've heard good and bad stories of young kids playing sports, so there is no one sure-fire answer. But one piece of advice I always give is that if both parents aren't convinced it's time, it's probably not.

ONE SHINING MOMENT

It was a big week last week in the Buzby household.

No, we didn't win the lottery, my snow blower still won't start, and I imagine my stock reports look just like yours.

It was senior night at the gym, and I, along with his mother, proudly accompanied Alex to center court to an ovation like he had never heard before.

He wasn't the star player on his high school basketball team, but thanks to his intelligent on-court decision-making and unselfish, blue-collar style of play, he was a fan favorite.

A play he made, or actually didn't, at the end of one of his last games put into context why he is always told that he plays the game the "right way." With less than twenty seconds to play and his team ahead by fifteen points, he got the ball after a rebound and streaked up the court. He could have easily gone in for a layup for another two points in the scorebook, or passed off to any of the other four players selfishly yelling for the ball to pad their own stats. But instead, he pulled up at half court, held onto the ball while the weary opposing players slowed with relief, and just let the time run out.

He once scored five goals in a hockey game, twenty points in a basketball game and struck out thirteen batters in a six-inning Little League game. But I can honestly say that it was that one unselfish play which made me the proudest.

During just his second season of competitive basketball when he was in middle school a coach told him that he should always continue to "play the game the right way." He was one of the only ones on that team who did. And, unfortunately, he was one of just a few who played sound fundamental basketball on this year's varsity team. It didn't go unnoticed by the fans on senior night as he was rewarded with an ovation.

When he held onto the ball and let time run out that previous game, a huge smile went across my face. It made me feel like he actually learned some of the important things about sports I tried to teach him from the very beginning. And not just how to shoot a basketball or swing a bat, but lessons that at the time he might not have understood — like when he was five years old and I wouldn't let him shoot any more after scoring four goals in the first half of a hockey game — but ones that he'll use in life now that his playing days are over.

As I stood with him at center court a rush of sports memories came back to me. Some of them were good, others not so good. But the most important thing about all of those memories is that we made them together; yes as coach and player, but more importantly, as father and son. Nothing can ever break up that team.

Age and time has now taken away the opportunity for us to play and coach on the same team. But what will never be forgotten are the memories we made along the way. We shared long drives to and from games, some spent silent after tough losses while others were animated after a big win. We spent time eating dinners on the road, either in our laps in the car or out with the team. And we had a few occasional long-distance tournament trips to memorable places.

During his playing years he played competitive roller hockey, soccer, ice hockey, lacrosse, baseball, golf and basketball. And as I stood there at center court and thought back to all of his teams, many of which I coached, I remembered several times when he felt like a champion.

That night at center court as he soaked in the applause and appreciation for a job well done, he once again felt like a champion.

And it was a moment I'll never forget.

WHO NEEDS A CAR

Riley turned one a couple weeks ago.

My wife and I started the tradition of writing him a letter on his birthday, each scribing our own to reflect the memories of the past year. We plan to do this each year until he's eighteen and then present them all to him on his birthday that year. I scoffed at the idea at first but then figured, heck, handing him a bunch of letters when he turns eighteen will be cheaper than buying him a new car.

Dear Riley,

Wow, what a difference a year makes. A year ago you came into our life and nothing has been the same since.

My mornings start off two hours earlier than they used to and the sports page gets read three days after games end, but the ninety minutes we spend alone together every morning before I take you to daycare is time I wouldn't trade for anything. It's treasured time that will continue for many years to come, when we might even be joined by a sibling. It's a time that I know will end someday, not by my choice, but by your maturation. I hope it takes forever.

Just as your days start with me, so do they end, during tubby time. This past year you went from a sponge bath in the sink to dunking balls in the hoop your older brother gave you for Christmas. My guess is next year at this time you'll want to experiment with the shower and tubby time will no longer be fun for me. Instead I'll peek in to make sure you really are washing and I'll spend as much time toweling off the floor as I will you.

I watched you go through each movement stage of your first year, from the "blob" stage, as your mother calls it, to now learning how to walk. We child-proofed the house as soon as you started crawling and I promised your mom we'd move the coffee table back as soon as you can navigate on two feet without toppling over. You learned it's better to be carried down the steps and that the oven drawer gets hot, and just what hot means. Mom and I learned a lot, too. Your future sibling will owe you a "Thanks, bro!"

I'll never forget your first summer and your first ride on the back of my bike. You won't either because you loved it so much you fell asleep halfway through it. You loved sitting on mommy's lap and watching your older brother and me play one-on-one at the end of each day. Someday it will be you and me, and I'll be even slower, if you can imagine that's possible.

You attended your first college football tailgate and watched your favorite baseball team make the playoffs for the first time in fifteen years. Your mother's favorite football team won the Super Bowl, and fortunately, you aren't old enough yet to know your favorite team is the Jets.

You can say you lived through the last year of steroids in baseball, and fortunately, you'll never remember it.

You're living through the primary election battle between, potentially, the first African-American President, or the first female in the Oval Office. And, of course, at your age you'd still rather watch Sesame Street than a political debate. You really are just like me.

Your mommy saved every slip from your first year at daycare. Why, I'm not sure. But as you'll soon learn, I never second guess Mommy. After all, it was her idea to write you a letter for your birthday. And I now think it's a great idea.

So in closing ...

Happy Birthday, Riley! One year down, a lifetime to go. I hope you enjoy every second of it. I know I sure will.

Love,
Daddy

THE EXPENSIVE LETTER

As parents we all want our kids' dreams to come true.

For my senior in high school that dream included attending the University of Delaware, and so when a big thick blue and gold envelope arrived at the house — compared to a smaller boring envelope perfectly sized for a rejection letter — the entire household breathed a sigh of relief.

Son number one had already been accepted and received a partial scholarship to another big school, but it wasn't the one he wanted. And even though I thought it might ultimately be a better fit for him for a variety of reasons, the fact that he dreamed of attending, and now will be, my alma mater brought with it a sense of pride.

In the weeks leading up to him receiving his notice, and as more and more of his friends and my friends' kids heard from their colleges of choice, I started rehearsing my "it's not the end of the world" speech just in case he did not get accepted. I was confident he would, if for no other reason than his academic accomplishments were similar, if not better, compared to others we knew who were already accepted. But as I told myself over and over during many sleep-interrupted nights, you never know for sure until that letter arrives.

Of course, now that he's in and it's official that he is going to attend the University of Delaware, I spent most of the first night after we found out he was accepted worrying about how he'll fare once he leaves the nest.

Some questions were simple. Will he meet friends? Will his current girlfriend, who will still be in high school, impede his social opportunities? Some were more serious. How will he do academically? Will he settle on a major that he not only likes, but one that will land him a job when he graduates? Have I instilled in him good enough morals and values to make wise decisions in sticky situations?

And then, of course, the easily-answered question: Will he miss me? Not.

I've already decided I'm going to try and be like my parents were — a common theme now that I'm a parent — when I went off to college as the first of three children to leave the nest, and let him become an adult.

I found friends. My left-behind high school girlfriend lasted three weeks, but it was my choice, not my parents', to move on. My parents encouraged me to pick a major I liked more than one I'd make a lot of money with, which I did. But of course, like many, my current job has nothing to do with that major. And I learned about college partying. After all, we all do.

I think what I learned more than anything during those first few months on campus was not only that you can mix colors in the washing machine if you wash on cold, but it was time to take advantage of the opportunity I had laid before me to get a college degree.

In other words, I have to start mentally preparing myself for September when he moves into the dorms and I won't talk to him every day. I'll have to try hard not to text him incessantly, and will try and understand that he won't be eager to come home on the weekends despite living less than ten miles away.

After all, thinking back, I would have loathed those things. Sorry, Mom and Dad, just reality … like when you went away to college, too.

I have to remember that he's no longer a little boy, but rather a young man. And although he still has a heck of a lot to learn, he's proven he's already learned a heck of a lot.

I won't agree with every decision he makes at college, and he won't agree when I don't. But my parents never stood in the way of my dreams, and I don't plan to stand in the way of his.

After all, as parents, all we want for our kids is for all of their dreams to come true.

One of my son's dreams just did.

THE PERFECT GIFT

I recently celebrated my forty-second birthday and received what I thought was the perfect gift from my wife and boys.

It wasn't a romantic night out or breakfast in bed. I don't have any more ugly ties than I did when I was forty-one, and I didn't have to make any more room in the garage for additional power tools that I might get hurt using.

Once I went through the polite routine of opening my cards first — if we are honest we never really outgrow wanting to rip right into presents — I was thrilled to realize the large box with a bow on it contained one very small item.

For my birthday I received tickets to a local show where ESPN's Tony Kornheiser and Michael Wilbon would be on stage bantering back and forth like they do nightly on "Pardon the Interruption." And the next surprise was that I was not going alone. And even better, I was not going with my wife and kids, even though I love them dearly.

Instead, I was heading out with two of my friends and was expected to go out and enjoy myself before the show, regardless of how many boys needed to be bathed or changed at home during the same time period.

Don't get me wrong, most of my absolute favorite memories involve doing things with my family. But once in a while, it's nice to do something with just the guys. As we get older, it happens less and less. And even when it does, we're often saddled with guilt that we are out of the house.

But this night was mine, and I planned to enjoy every minute of it.

We started at the local pub, conveniently located within walking distance of the show. Simply put, rounds of pints could safely be ordered instead of the usual bottleneck. With the March Madness first-round games playing on every television, all of a sudden the fact that one of my Final Four teams got bounced earlier in the day — all but eliminating me from any chance of declaring myself Bracketologist of the Year — seemed completely trivial and irrelevant.

Once at the show, we enjoyed the humorous banter between the sports celebrities as much as any game any of us had ever attended with our kids. It was a chance to sit and enjoy the action without having to run to the concession stand or the bathroom with a little one, only to return to find out the play of the game just happened. Is there anything worse than hearing the loudest roar of the day from the home crowd as you stand at the urinal?

None of us heard "I want to go home" from the seat next to us, and the only time my cell phone beeped was when a jealous friend sitting at home with two kids on his lap sent me a text message with tournament updates.

When the show painfully ended and I finally did arrive home back to reality, I checked in on my two youngest boys, both snuggled in bed sound asleep.

My last stop was to my teenager's room, where I found him snoring with the light on and television blaring (I am trying to figure out how to move the electric meter into his room), cell phone laying on his pillow, and his bracket crumpled up next to a pencil snapped in two. It was then I was reminded of one of my all-time favorite birthday gifts.

The painted tin can full of various writing utensils is something I look at every day at work, and when I do, I can still see the proud smile on my oldest son's face as he watched me take the wrapping paper off his fine work of art (he knew even at that young age not to bother giving a card). It was a look that no picture or words could give justice, but one that I'll never forget.

It was a nice reminder that the so-called perfect birthday gift doesn't always have to involve loved ones, but more often than not, the unforgettable ones do.

WHO'S DOING THE CHORES

After procrastinating for weeks, I was all fired up and ready to head out and get some weeding done. But then the toddler woke up. Thank goodness.

I decided I'd wait and weed one night during the week, when my fifteen-year-old son wants to be out front shooting hoops near the flowerbed. I could still count that as father-son time, right?

Then I started thinking that maybe he should be weeding with me. Or maybe he should be weeding by himself and I should be practicing my foul shots for our weekly competition.

Which led me to wonder: When do we start having our kids do the outdoor chores that we dads (and moms) traditionally have done?

I actually don't mind doing yard work. I'm not handy around the house, so cutting the grass, trimming and pulling weeds are all chores that I find great satisfaction completing, in part, I suppose, because I don't have to call a repairman to undo my damage.

And of course, someone has to clean up after the dog. Repairmen don't do that.

Don't get me wrong, I'd much rather play golf than do chores, although the way I play, that should be considered a chore. But when our grass gets to the height that makes the rough at the U.S. Open seem short and there are more weeds than stones in the beds, I know it's unavoidably time to mow, trim and weed.

Growing up, I never once was asked to cut the grass, weed the flowerbeds or trim anything. I'm not sure who cleaned up after the dog, just that it wasn't me. Dad told us he loved doing yard work. Mom says it was because he couldn't hear us kids fighting over the noise of the lawnmower.

My guess is my weekly outdoor chores are similar to most of yours. The grass needs to be cut, some weeds need to be pulled and trimming needs to be done. If I had to rank these three chores in order of my preference, it would be mowing, trimming and weeding.

I asked my son what his first choice would be. His reply was, "Not to help at all." My guess is your child would give you a similar response.

But I think it's important for teenagers of both genders to start helping with chores outside the house as soon as they safely can. Lawn mowing and trimming can be dangerous if a child is not physically ready to handle the equipment. Weeding and cleaning the beds is much safer, but also more tedious and less likely to get completed to our satisfaction. After all, are you ever really completely finished weeding? Just when you think you are, you see one more, and then the next morning, many more weeds peeking through the area you swear you just cleaned out. And this is after you spread expensive weed killer all over the place.

So the question I ponder is with whether I should tell my son what chores he is going to do or not make him do any at all? Or should I meet him halfway?

I've decided to meet him halfway. I'm going to let him choose which one of the three outdoor chores he wants to do each week. He can even rotate them if he wants. But he won't be paid. I consider this to be part of him earning his keep. If he asks why we don't pay him to cut the grass, my reply will be, "Because we don't ask you to leave a tip at the dinner table."

He will balk at the thought of having to do anything outside that doesn't involve a ball or have wheels, and hate doing it even more for free. But in the long run, like any childhood lesson, hopefully it will pay off when he's a dad.

Someday, he'll have to decide when to turn the mower over to his kids. I'm not sure if he'll heed my advice or not, but hopefully he'll look back on this and realize why I'm doing it.

And he'll probably also discover, as I have, that dog poop doesn't just disappear.

A PERFECT MOTHER'S DAY

If I left it up to my sons as to what to do for Mommy for Mother's Day, my guess is she'd unwrap a toy car, be served cookies in bed for breakfast, and sit down to boiled hot dogs and applesauce for dinner.

Her special card would have Elmo on the front cover and the "Barney" theme song would blare when it was opened.

If I ask her what she wants, her reply will be, "Nothing, I already have everything I need with you and the boys."

Translation: "I don't care, but it better not involve me taking the boys anywhere by myself for quality time with them while you play golf."

I've decided I'm going to get up with both kids tomorrow morning. The one I can't nurse will get a bottle, while the older one — who, by the way, recently discovered his own nipples — "breastfeeds" his teddy bear.

Rather than go out and stand in line at a restaurant with hundreds of other fathers who are listening to their restless kids pleading to go home, this dad plans to make his wife's favorite breakfast from scratch (Bisquick is scratch, right?).

After breakfast, instead of the usual Sunday morning routine of me claiming to have to go out and cut the grass (alone) for the second time of the weekend, I'm going to send my wife out for a walk … without a stroller.

After lunch we'll go to our favorite park, where she can play with Riley while I sit under a tree as Tyler sleeps in his stroller.

We'll return home for the boys' naps and it will be up to my wife whether or not she wants to take a nap herself, go out somewhere alone, watch the Food Network, or maybe participate in an activity with me that spurned the onset of motherhood to begin with (wink wink). I'm confident at this point I'll be sent out to cut the grass, whether it needs it or not.

Dinner will be her choice. I grill a mean hot dog, but other than that and pancakes, anything I might prepare will be a downer compared to her gourmet cooking. If she's smart, she'll choose takeout.

Riley will then present her with the boys' gift: a mouse pad with a collage of the boys' pictures.

While this might seem simple and "cheap" for Mother's Day, knowing my wife like only I do, she'll appreciate that much more than a day at the spa (she would view that as punishment), a Phillies T-shirt (she's a Mets fan), over-priced flowers, or the toy car that Riley suggested when he pulled it out of the cereal box the other morning.

With the mouse pad, she can look at it and be reminded every morning when she goes to work — bothered that her boys are off to daycare — that she has two beautiful boys that she's doing a spectacular job nurturing even when she isn't with them. Besides, I couldn't figure out a cute way to put on the mouse pad that she has to work so we get her family benefits.

I also ordered her a card that has a picture of the boys happily playing together on the front of it. It will be for her to look at when they start using each other for punching bags. I'll have them both scribble on it as a keepsake.

It's another perfect gift for her because she loves keeping keepsakes. So much so that each boy has his daily daycare report from his first year of life tucked away in a memory box. Their future wives will be thrilled to someday read what their husbands ate for breakfast and lunch each day … and if and what time they pooped.

Speaking of memories, when we sit back and think about it, most of our fondest memories during childhood occurred with Mom around, and usually, because of her.

And for that reason and so many more we don't just give our moms a gift on this special day, but more importantly, we celebrate one of life's most precious gifts - moms themselves.

OUTTA HERE

Earlier this afternoon I sat along the right-field foul line at my son's high school baseball game. His team had a two-run lead in the bottom of the second inning and the ninth batter was at the plate.

This ninth batter had been struggling for the last few games, slowly dipping toward the bottom of the batting order until he could go no lower.

He was a singles hitter and a reliable bunter. And built like one.

There were runners on first and second with nobody out, an ideal bunting situation at any level of baseball. I anticipated watching this player lay down a superb bunt to move the runners along and allow the top of the order to knock them in.

The pitcher wound up and delivered. Instead of squaring to bunt, the left-handed batter swung with perfect Ken Griffey Jr.-like form, and all of a sudden the ball came soaring toward me in right field. A huge smile came over my face as I realized it was definitely going over the right fielder's head.

I thought to myself, "Is there any way this slight-of-build ninth hitter, who had hit nothing but singles all season, can hit one out of the park?"

The right fielder stopped as the ball landed and began rolling on the other side of the fence. The batter went into his never-before-performed-live home run trot. It was the same trot he had probably practiced countless times during backyard games.

His coach let out a holler as his shocked teammates poured out of the dugout to greet him at the plate. He was beaming with confidence.

116

I retrieved the ball and after the game wandered over to find the player. I handed him the ball and shook his hand.

He smiled ear-to-ear, and said, "Thanks, Dad."

I had a tear in my eye ... similar to the one now as I type.

He might never hit another home run again, and that won't matter to me. Because even if he does, it will never generate the feeling I had earlier today when I handed him that ball.

It's a feeling that can't really be described ... other than maybe with a tear in an eye.

HANDS AT TEN AND TWO O'CLOCK

It seems like just yesterday I let go of the seat and watched my oldest son, now sixteen, proudly zoom off in the distance on his two-wheeler. It was one of the most exciting times of his youth.

But last week, I sat beside him in the passenger seat — my fists clenched in my pocket — as he drove me home from the Department of Motor Vehicles with his temporary driving permit officially in hand (actually, in his wallet - both hands on the wheel at all times). His smile was similar to that day on his bike eleven years ago.

It's now my job to prepare him for his first solo drive. He'll beg, badger and plead to drive every time we get in the car together, and most likely even be willing to go with me on errands he'd typically decline. He'll actually get to see where I take the recycling, dump the yard waste, and put gas in the car.

I've decided one of the most nerve-wracking times in any parent's life is that inevitable task of teaching your child to drive. It feels like we no sooner put them on the kindergarten bus and then they are arguing with us that they should be able to drive the family car to school rather than take that same long yellow limousine they were so excited to board back in grade school.

My son's generous offer the other day was about how much easier my life would be if he could drive to school. He even offered to drive his stepmother to the delivery room in November so he could have the car that day, which I haven't suggested yet to her for fear of inducing an early labor.

118

There's probably not a more exciting time in any teenager's life than when he finally gets behind the wheel. I remember how excited I was counting down the days until I could drive. Little did I know I was really counting down the days until I became my younger brother's chauffeur.

My son's youthful ignorance reared its head when he asked if my insurance costs would go up. My laugh in response answered that question for him. And then that first thought of panic reached my throat when I realized the answer to that question, and I wasn't laughing any more.

As far as practicing with him, I can tell you one thing for sure, and that's that we will spend more quality time together with him behind the wheel than we ever did with me behind it. There are no hand-held games distracting him, the radio is not just turned down, it's off, and I think he actually feels like he has to talk to me as a thank you for letting him drive.

When he is driving, I try to make a point to be nothing but positive and limit my advice to the really important things. That usually lasts until the car is in reverse and we begin our descent down the driveway. I try to think back to my days of practicing with mom and dad and they were pretty positive. Or at least they disguised their rising blood pressure pretty well.

I try to emphasize little things like sitting up straight and keeping two hands on the wheel, that he should never be on his cell phone or have the radio blaring. He hasn't been bold enough yet to point out I should listen to my own advice.

Unfortunately, cars aren't built like they are in the amusement park kiddy rides with steering wheels on both sides. And I don't have the emergency brake like the driver's education car.

Two positives are we don't own a stick shift, so my back and neck get a break right off the bat, and he doesn't have to learn how to parallel park a station wagon like I did.

So now I have six months to do everything in my power to make him the best driver he can be, just like my parents did with me.

Fortunately, he's a pretty good driver. But even that doesn't guarantee he'll never get in an accident or see flashing lights approach from behind. There's living proof of that in the passenger seat next to him.

But in six months, I'll watch him pull out of the driveway without me by his side, and just like I beamed as he pedaled away from me, I'll smile as I watch him drive off into the horizon.

And then I'll worry like hell.

CURING WRITER'S BLOCK

If a man is lucky, he gets to go through the first year of his child's life once in a lifetime. I've now been lucky enough to do it for the third time.

As I sat down to type a letter to my one-year-old son, I struggled to come up with words. Call it writer's block I guess, but regardless, I just couldn't seem to figure out exactly what I wanted to say. But then, at a social event just the other day, it hit me. Or, I should say, Tyler smiled at me ...

Dear Tyler:

It was your beautiful smile drenched by alligator tears that struck a chord in my heart unlike any other moment during your first year of life.

While at a football tailgate a good friend of ours picked you up as I disappeared to tend to something else, and all of a sudden I heard you burst into tears. I quickly came back around the corner and the smile that lit up your face just melted my heart.

I look back on your first year of life with so many wonderful memories. There was the day we brought you home and your brother tried to send you back. There were the sleepless nights followed by some nap-less days. And of course the memories of you reaching the typical baby milestones.

But of all your moments that I enjoyed and will treasure forever this past year, and there were many, none

121

was more special to me than the other day at the tailgate when in your own little way you unknowingly showed me just how special our relationship as father and son will always be.

And I'm not suggesting I didn't think about or realize this before now. It's just that in the hustle and bustle of the past year, which included making your almost three-year-old brother still feel special while helping your oldest brother manage his last years of high school, I think I'm guilty of just trying to get through each day rather than really appreciating what having a third son means to me.

Ever since the day you were born I've referred to you often as the final member of my golfing foursome. You are my "littlest guy."

But what I really haven't spent enough time thinking about is just how lucky I am to be a daddy for the third time, and to be so to a son who is so good your mom swears if we weren't so old you wouldn't be the last.

So when I saw you smile and your eyes light up as I came back "into your life" after being gone for only a brief second, but for what probably seemed like an eternity in your little world, that smile not only melted my heart, but reignited my thoughts about how, as my third and final son, you always will be my "special littlest guy."

That little flex of your dimple-loaded grin reminded me what I already knew but had let slip into routine: That being a daddy is the most wonderful feeling in the world. And in this case not just any daddy, but yours.

We'll have a ton of storybook-like father-son moments ahead when I'll look at you and see you smile again. They will be moments we'll both remember forever.

122

But unlike those times yet to come, this one particular smile is one that you'll never recall, and that's why I wanted to write to you about it. It's the type of memory only a daddy can relate to, and one you won't understand until you experience it yourself. So for now, you'll have to trust me when I tell you, it meant the world to me.

When you finally do get a chance to read this letter, what I hope you'll gleam from my words is how that one smile, witnessed on a cold football Saturday, warmed my heart in a way words never could.

And unlike that smile, which hopefully I've somewhat accurately described in words, what I'll never, ever be able to express to you on paper is just how much having you as my son means to me.

Love, Dad

MOST IMPORTANT CALL OF THE DAY

Several weeks ago, I was sitting at my wife's baby shower listening to my cousin's wife talk about life at their house since the infestation. Not a bug infestation, but a kids' one.

She said it took her a while to make her husband realize that he was now just an assistant coach on the team called Family.

I'm not sure he was ever the head coach, but am pretty sure at one point he was at least the co-coach. But now he has been demoted to assistant coach. I'm not sure even he's convinced of this yet, but after hearing a few stories, I am.

So I have to ask myself, with the birth of my second child am I headed for the same relegation? Am I done calling plays in my own house? At least ones that count. I'm sure I'll still have the freedom to decide how to arrange the trash cans and what night to cut the grass, sort of like the assistant coach in charge of arranging the chairs during timeouts.

I'm sure the scene is similar in households all over the country where mom is home all day with the kids and dad arrives after work, just like a visiting team in a foreign arena playing in the last quarter of a very long game. He walks through the front door and the kids bombard him, asking questions that they hope have different answers than the ones they've been getting all day from Mom. Mom no sooner has them settled down in front of the television, and Dad storms in ready to play kickball ... in the house.

Mom has laid out the entire game plan for the evening as far as dinner, dessert, baths and television, and Dad comes home and diagrams a new play. Instead of dinner, bath and television, Dad decides to "help" Mom out and treat the family at the local ice cream parlor and eliminate the kids' favorite shows to give his wife an earlier break.

After this announcement, all hell breaks loose. One kid is tearing around squealing with delight anticipating his favorite cone, while the other is furious that her favorite show is on after the newly announced bedtime. Dad is trying to quiet one child and calm the other while Mom comes running in to help. Meanwhile, the water boils over, the dog gets stepped on, and the spill-proof juicy cup gets thrown in anger onto the white carpet and the lid pops off.

Great start to the fourth quarter. Way to go, coach.

One thing I never heard growing up in my house was, "Just wait until your father gets home and he'll deal with you." Or, "Your father will make that decision when he gets home." My mom needed no help dealing out discipline or establishing the evening strategy.

Nor will my wife. Consequences will be handed down swiftly, reasonably and cannot simply be overturned when I walk through the door, or I'll be benched. Evening routines will be developed with thought and tactics based on the plays of the day prior to my arrival.

A friend of mine once told me that the most important conversation he and his wife have the entire day is on the cell phone before he arrives home. They discuss the ups and downs of their own day, but most importantly, the kids' days. They discuss what has happened, who did what to whom, along with the consequences already dealt out, and what the routine will be for the rest of the night.

This way there are no surprises, misinterpretations or, to borrow a basketball phrase, no flagrant foul-ups by Dad. And there is absolutely no second-guessing the head coach.

I can't help but think that if every set of parents took just five minutes before Dad (or Mom in some households) arrives home to discuss the plays of the day and the game plan for the rest of the night, it would make evenings all over the country a little more peaceful.

There would be fewer timeouts, fewer fouls and most importantly, everyone would win.

HALLOWEEN IS SCARY

The other morning my wife and I were discussing whether or not Halloween is absolutely the dumbest holiday of the year. We had just purchased our infant's dragon costume that cost more than dinner out and he'll wear for about ten minutes and almost immediately outgrow.

From a teacher's standpoint, we've determined it basically eliminates three days of the academic year, even though the kids are in the classrooms all three of those days.

There is so much excitement the day before Halloween that the kids aren't focused. And the day of? Well, forget it. I still haven't figured out why the classes just don't party all day, and not try to justify waiting until after lunch. And just when you think the day after will be normal, the kids arrive still sugared up from the night before and tired from being out so late. It's the worst combination for optimal learning. You might as well give the kids the day after Halloween off, except that the parents can't wait to send them to school.

It never fails there are at least two kids in every class that arrive to the school Halloween parade without a costume. It might be for a variety of reasons including the parents can't afford one, maybe they forgot, or they don't believe in the tradition for religious reasons. But regardless, a few kids without costumes feel completely out of place while everyone else is donning their masks and parading around the hallways.

And speaking of costumes, how much money is wasted each year on them? There are stores that open just for the month of October. The winner of every contest is usually the kid who either has the most creative mom who can sew or the richest parents who can use a plastic card to purchase a winning costume.

I used to abhor the houses where the owners asked you to do a trick. It was like I was going to make something disappear or pull a rabbit out of my candy bag. What I dislike even more, now as an adult, are the high school-aged kids who put a mask on and race all over the neighborhoods trying to get as much free candy as they can, barely stopping long enough to say, "Thanks." And often they don't even live in the neighborhood.

And then there's our dog. Every time someone rings the doorbell, the dog goes nuts. He tears around the house barking like crazy, trying to get out. Not so much because he wants to attack anyone, but because he's smart enough to know the front door will be open and leads to uncharted territory for him. So from dusk until the front light goes out, my house is nothing but noise. Just as the most recent trick-or-treaters disappear from the dog's sight, the next bunch arrive. You'd think the dog would go hoarse. Nope.

Every year, we are invited to a Halloween party for adults only. It's with a group of friends that we'd have a great time with, but we're expected to dress up. So we don't go.

I guess you could say my attitude about Halloween stinks. Well, time for an attitude adjustment.

As my wife was showing me Riley's costume, I started thinking back to my Halloweens as a child. As a kid with the world's biggest sweet tooth, it was probably my favorite. I tried to get as much candy as possible and even backtracked to a few houses who gave away my favorites. I never really cared what my costume was — Batman one year, a cowboy the next — because to me, the most important part was the candy. Just like most kids.

I loved carrying my costume to school knowing that the afternoon party there was just the beginning of, in my eyes, the greatest night of the year.

I guess after re-reading my rants about this upcoming holiday, what I need to realize first and foremost is that Halloween is not designed to entertain us adults. It's clearly a holiday for kids.

And that's what I need to remember when I head out the door with my little dragon on the last day of October. I can't let my attitude spoil it for him, other trick-or-treaters, or even my dog.

It's also probably the only year that Riley won't be able to verbally explain to his mother that the reason we were out so long is because we back-tracked to every house giving out Reese's Peanut Butter Cups.

SHOULD PARENTS COACH

My five-year-old nephew announced that he wanted to play soccer this fall "but only if Daddy is the head coach."

I'm sure he's not alone, as it's not unusual for a child to see a friend's dad or mom coaching a team and wants to be in the same situation. Or your child might just want you there for security.

But what if you don't want to coach? Or don't have the experience to do so? Or, as is often the case, don't have the time to commit.

I made sure that the first team my son played on was one I didn't coach. I helped out during the practices whenever asked, just like many of the other parents. But when it came time to play the games, I was in the bleachers.

I did this so that when I was able to be an official head coach — and I have been several times after that initial season — it would be because I wanted to do it and had the time to do the job correctly, not because I had to in order for my child to want to play.

If your child is claiming he'll only play if you coach, it might be too early to start him participating in team sports. Or if he's older and knows you won't coach, he might be using his demand as a way to get out of playing. Every child should want to play to enjoy the sport, be with friends, and of course, learn a little bit about the game. That should happen regardless of whether mom or dad coaches.

Giving in to your child and agreeing to coach might be setting a bad precedent by setting up expectations that eventually might be impossible to meet for one reason or another.

That being said, a compromise might be to consider the role of an assistant coach, either officially or unofficially. Or do as I did this past spring and be the official scorekeeper. You can promise your child — and the head coach — that you will be at as many practices and games as you can, but have to leave the head coaching duties to another parent because you can't make all of them.

Handling the situation this way gives your child the reassurance that you will be there most of the time, but the realization that there will be some practices and games that you just can't attend. It's still important for your child to realize he is expected to attend practices on the days when you aren't there, and my guess is once the season starts, you'll find he wants to anyway.

With most kids, provided they enjoy the sports activity, the hardest part is just getting them involved on that first team. Once they get started and realize how much fun youth sports can be, a parent's presence becomes less and less important.

Of course, as parents, sometimes it's hard to face that fact once we are not needed. But when we do, the youth sports experience becomes more fulfilling for everyone involved, most importantly, for your child.

LET YOUR KIDS PLAY

During the summer months, we parents probably play outside with our children more than at any other time of the year. Unlike during the school year, days are longer, temperatures are warmer, evening commitments fewer, and there is no homework to complete or spelling tests to study for.

Like a lot of youth sports parents, I find myself trying to coach my child while we're playing in the backyard.

My son wants to play goalie when we play roller hockey. I want him to practice his stick-handling skills.

He wants to play soccer, which is a sport he doesn't even play in a league. I want us to play basketball since he actually belongs to a league.

He wants to play Whiffle ball. I want him to let me pitch baseballs to him.

I try to work on technique. He just wants to have fun.

I get stressed out when he doesn't want to listen. He gets upset when I won't stop coaching.

Children need to play and it needs to be fun. If it's not fun, they will lose interest. Playing is important at any age. How many of us would play the recreational sports we do if every time we swung the club or racquet someone was correcting our technique?

Summer is the perfect time to start letting your child dictate how to spend his spare time playing. Of course, that is as long as it's safe.

I asked my son why he plays soccer at recess since it's a sport he does not play in a formal league. His response was, "Because it's fun."

During recess, there are no coaches, no parents, no officials and no pressure. Kids can make up the teams and the rules to make sure they have fun.

The same should happen at home, and not just during the summer months.

If you're wondering why all of a sudden your child does not want to play basketball with you, think back to the last few times you were outside playing together. Did you spend more time coaching than just being a parent? Did you dictate what the two of you would play and how it should be played? If so, you may have taken the fun out of your child's play.

The next time you go outside to play with your child, try to make an honest effort to let him or her decide what you'll play and what the rules will be. Don't correct, explain or demonstrate unless you're asked. You might be surprised how much fun you'll have together.

And the best part is that the next night most likely your child will want you to play again.

SAYING GOODBYE TO A FURRY FRIEND

One of the hardest decisions I ever had to make was when to put my seventeen-year-old mutt to sleep a few weeks ago.

The decision-making process began when my once active pup struggled to stand for long periods of time, paced as she fought the effects of Alzheimer's, couldn't hear anything other than a high-pitched whistle, and was becoming less and less reliable to make it outside before an accident occurred. All of these criteria, based on books and internet blogs, are signs that it might be time.

However, she ate well, seemed to be in no pain, had not started snapping at people, and still wanted to be around any human being in the house rather than lay alone. According to those same resources, signs it might not have been time.

I tried to forget the cost and sometimes hassle — a middle-of-the-night carpet cleaning — associated with keeping her alive. I thought that was only fair. So money and frustration aside, how would I know when it was really time to make that difficult decision?

As I saw her back leg give out while she ate, forcing her to finish the last morsels while lying down, I thought it was time. And then I saw the food gone from the dish, her get excited for dessert and still have the energy to try and steal her doggy brother's treat as well.

As I picked up the trail of poop from the kitchen to the doggie door, I thought it was time. But then I watched the next few times as she scampered rather quickly for a dog her age down the ramp and out the door to take care of her business.

As I carried her up long flights of steps I thought back to her bounding all over the house during her younger years, and I thought it must be time. But then I watched her peacefully sleep next to our bed, snuggled up in her blankets, through the night, perfectly content.

When I would come into the house and have to wake her to announce that I was home rather than see her jumping up and down with excitement, I thought it was time. But then I would see her following me around the house everywhere just begging to be pet or held or handed a treat, just like when she was a pup.

So I struggled as to when to make the ultimate decision.

I don't think there are any easy answers to this question. What I do know is that I'm sure far too many people selfishly wait too long to make the decision, or don't wait long enough because of the aggravation and cost.

And then it happened, like a good friend suggested it would. One morning I watched her painfully crawl out of bed, not make it outside in time, and then literally just lay there pleading for help in her own painful way. It was at that moment that I knew it was time.

Later that day my wife and I made that excruciating trip to the veterinarian. We both had a good cry and said goodbye, and then we held her as her heart came to rest.

She looked so peaceful, so pain-free. As much as I ached, I knew she no longer did ... and that's when I knew for sure that it really was the right time.

TAKING AIM AT A BIRDIE

Picture this: Six young boys on a lakefront beach standing next to a volleyball net with two rackets and a shuttlecock, which is a birdie for you casual badminton players. And there I am sitting on a lounge chair watching. Let the games begin!

It was a perfect start to a relaxing vacation. I sat and watched as these boys embarked on organizing a badminton tournament. It was single elimination and they declared a winner about every fifteen minutes before starting the tournament all over again. The rules were simple.

You can serve overhand or underhand from anywhere you want on your side of the net.

If the birdie goes over the net and lands anywhere on the other side, including out of bounds in the sand, in the lake, on a boat or on a rock, it's good.

If the birdie hits the net at any time you take it over. No questions asked or arguments made.

If the birdie is on your side after the point, you serve it.

Play to one-hundred by tens.

Winner stays, loser swims.

Everyone was having a great time. Win or lose, all you could hear was laughter and cheering from every player. I was amazed that six children, ranging in age from seven to twelve could all get along so well. There was no arguing, no tears, and no name-calling.

And then the youth coach got involved (that would be me). Why not teach them the real badminton rules? But keep it simple. Here were my suggestions:

Serve underhand only. Use boundaries. Play to six to keep the games short. Serve three times and then let your opponent serve three times.

The players were leery at first but soon all agreed. They seemed to be excited to know the real rules of the game. I proudly returned to my chair having taught these eager boys the right way to play badminton.

I was just getting back into my book when all of a sudden the arguing started.

"It's in!" "It's out!" "You already served three times." Etc., etc.

Soon the tears started flowing and one player stormed off the beach because he wasn't able to serve it underhand and get it over the net.

Now, just one hour into my vacation, I seemed to have the entire beach in an upheaval. I quickly suggested they go back to their old rules. They refused, insisting on playing the "right way."

I sheepishly walked away from the arguing and crying and headed to the end of the dock. I jumped in the lake. It was a simple jump. No cannon ball or swan dive. There were no rules and no judges there to critique or correct me.

As I turned and looked back to the beach, I thought to myself that maybe the boys were playing the right way before I got involved, because it was their way. Sometimes kids just need to be left alone to make the rules and play their way.

Despite not being perfect, my jump in the lake felt great.

Unfortunately, it was about an hour too late.

WHAT DO DADS REALLY KNOW

I recently read a column about what moms know best and it got me thinking: What do we dads know?

Dads know the snooze button was made to be pressed more than once and the more you press it the more likely mom will get up first. Dads also know that when the baby is crying in the middle of the night he really wants Mommy, and that breastfeeding is the absolute best invention ever.

We know kids prefer Lucky Charms to Cheerios and that a big piece of leftover birthday cake for breakfast is no different than having a doughnut.

Dads know if the toothbrush is wet the paste must have been used and no further inspection needs to happen.

Fathers know to have a good excuse prepared ahead of time as to why we can't chaperone the overnight field trip and another one ready for when we're asked to help with the school Halloween party.

We know our kids would prefer to miss first-period math class for an orthodontist appointment instead of baseball practice after school.

Dads know how to use the washer as long as colors can be mixed and the cold water dial used. We know how to fold, too, except for bras. I still haven't figured those out. And we know our underwear comes out of the drawer the same no matter how it's put in.

We know we are supposed to aim in the bathroom, we just aren't always good at it.

Fathers know what aisle the Oreos are in and that the kids won't miss the wheat bread as long as there is white. We know not to tell our

138

wives we really stopped for milk at the Speedy Mart and paid double what we would have at the grocery store just so we could get home in time for the start of the game. And the smart dads know to throw the coupons out if they aren't used rather than admit forgetfulness.

We solve tantrums with candy and disagreements with bribes.

We count french fries as vegetables and ice cream as a serving from the dairy food group. We know better than to complain about what is being served at home, if it's put on the table later than expected, or if it's not quite as hot as it should be.

Dads remember the first hit, the first high-five and the first time our child prefers to watch a game instead of cartoons. We remember our wife's birthday when our mom reminds us and our mom's birthday when our wife does the same. We could pick out our kids' teachers' names if given a multiple-choice list.

We seem to know how to schedule important meetings on the days the kids have to stay home sick from school.

Dads are great at pretending we know exactly what gift was purchased for which child on holidays or birthdays.

We know we screwed up when two of the same issue of Sports Illustrated arrive. And we are smart enough not to start the subscription around the time the swimsuit issue comes out.

We know when to ask for help finding something, usually after we've created a disaster looking for it.

We know reorganizing the pantry is off limits and that if something falls out of the freezer when we open it, most likely it's our fault for not putting it back correctly the last time we were in there. It doesn't stop us from doing it again, but it's good we know it's our fault.

We know how to inconspicuously drink directly from the orange juice carton and, of course, leave the empty one in the fridge as a reminder that we are now out of it.

Dads know it's more important to have the favorite team shirt on after a big win than a perfectly ironed generic one. We also know that moms care more than the kids or us dads that clothes match.

Fathers know that bedtime is actually when the final buzzer sounds and that bath time has more to do with time spent in the water than the amount of soap dispensed on the body.

After re-reading this, all I can say is, thank goodness for moms ... and of course, us dads.

ABOUT THE AUTHOR

Jon Buzby is an award-winning writer who has also written "Coaching Kids: It's More than X's and O's" and "Raising a Sports Fanatic." He lives in Bear, Delaware.

www.ingramcontent.com/pod-product-compliance
Lightning Source LLC
Chambersburg PA
CBHW060508030426
42337CB00015B/1803